The History of the Incas

Alfred Métraux

THE HISTORY OF THE INCAS

Translated from the French by George Ordish

SCHOCKEN BOOKS · NEW YORK

First SCHOCKEN PAPERBACK edition 1970
10 9 8 7   85 86 87 88
Published by arrangement with Pantheon Books

Copyright © 1969 by Random House, Inc.

Library of Congress Catalog Card No. 68–20890

Originally published in French under the title *Les Incas.*
Copyright © 1961 by Editions du Seuil.

Manufactured in the United States of America
ISBN 0–8052–0248–X

Acknowledgments

Alfred Métraux wishes to thank personally his colleagues and friends, MM. H. Reichlen of the Musée de l'homme and J. Murra of Vassar College, who generously assisted him with their advice. He expresses his gratitude to MM. Gerdt Kutscher, K. G. Izikowitz, and to Madame Lobsiger-Dellenbach for having kindly provided a large choice of objects from their collections, and also to the librarians of the Musée de l'homme and UNESCO for their help in his research.

Contents

Illustrations

Photo Credits

Archaeological Museum of the University of Trujillo, Peru: p. 34.

Archives A. Métraux: pp. 4, 16, 21, 26, 74, 109, 116, 152, 158, 163, 165, 167, 172, 173, 187.

Bibliothèque Nationale (Editions du Seuil): pp. 8, 9, 13, 14, 49.

René Burri/Magnum: p. 188.

Guillen: pp. xiii, 31, 32, 43, 80, 81, 101, 175.

Institut d'ethnographie, Geneva: p. 143.

Musée de l'homme, Paris: pp. 61, 75, 77, 91, 121, 199.

Museum of Ethnography, Berlin: pp. vii, 141.

Museum of Ethnography, Göteborg, Sweden: p. 129.

Henri Reichlen: pp. 22, 28, 50, 59, 67, 68, 72, 83, 88, 96, 132, 134, 139, 146, 147.

Staatl Museum für Völkerkunde, Munich: pp. 3, 39, 78, 104, 122, 151, 203.

Pierre Verger: pp. 35, 62, 65, 92, 102, 130, 144, 176, 184, 185, 192, 193, 195.

The History of the Incas

The Inca Mirage

On the evening of November 16, 1532, the Inca Atahuallpa was pulled from his litter, though it was surrounded by his guards, and made prisoner by Francisco Pizarro. His army, cut to pieces by a handful of horsemen, was lost in the night. In scarcely three hours the power of the most powerful state of pre-Columbian America was broken forever. The fall of the Inca empire preceded the death of a civilization regarded as remarkable even by the rough adventurers who destroyed it.

The ambush which opened the door for the Spaniards to the riches of Peru was the end of a long search. From the beginning of the sixteenth century the Spaniards, aware of the "joyfull newes," had been on the track of an Eldorado somewhere to the south, beyond the mountains and the forests; and from that time on they had flocked to "the golden coast" in ever increasing numbers. According to tradition Balboa was the first to hear of this mysterious country, before he discovered the Pacific and took possession of it in the king's name. He was with Comagre, who was a cacique from Darien near the Gulf of Urabá, when a

3

Inca seen through the eyes of the Romantic period

quarrel broke out between his companions over the division of some gold. On seeing this the cacique's son knocked the balance down, spilling its precious contents onto the ground, and said, "Christians, why do you quarrel about so insignificant a matter? If your thirst for gold is so great that you leave your own homes and disturb innocent peaceful people in order to find it, then I could show you countries where your desires would be fully satisfied."

On being questioned the young man told them that to conquer that land they would have to be in force, and to reach another sea, the Pacific, which, "having crossed, they would see the quantity of gold those people had and the golden vessels they used for eating and drinking."

When Vasco Nuñez de Balboa reached the shores of the Pacific (1513), the remarks of the Darien cacique were confirmed by a local chief of Tumnaco. This man, after describing the wonders of the "kings of gold," added that there they used certain animals as beasts of burden, and he drew an outline on the ground that was sufficiently accurate to enable the Spaniards to recognize a "sheep," which indeed the llamas and alpacas of Peru somewhat resemble.

At Panama in 1515, there was talk of nothing else but this unknown land, already called "Peru" from the name of a river in south Colombia and an Indian chief with whom the sailors had been in touch. When Pizarro and his companions actually discovered the Inca empire the custom of calling the place "Peru" from this obscure little stream had taken root, and the native name of *Tahuantin-suyu,* or the four quarters, was disregarded.

So widespread was the fame of the great Andean empire that its existence was known not only in Panama but throughout the continent, with the possible exception of distant Tierra del Fuego. While the Spaniards in Panama and the West Indies were eagerly absorbing rumors of the Eldorado to be found on the other side of the continent, the Portuguese on the coast of Brazil were hearing the same stories and were as impressed by them. In 1508, scarcely eight years after the fortuitous discovery of Brazil by Cabral, the captain of a reconnaissance ship sent out by a Portuguese shipowner had come back from Brazil with news that in the interior there was "a mountain people with rich

armor, made of plates of fine gold, covering the breast and head."
Not far from the spot where he had landed another sailor obtained from stark-naked Indians using stone axes and tools of wood and bone, "a silver ax and bits of metal the color of brass which did not tarnish."

The Portuguese who had obtained this "welcome news of Eldorado" had no doubt reached the southern coast of Brazil, then inhabited by the Carios, a tribe belonging to the Guarani Indians of Paraguay, who had long been in contact with the Incas, who supplied them with metal artifacts. Like all Stone Age people, they hankered after such goods, and in order to get them would even venture into the "green hell" of the Chaco, which lay between them and the Andes, where copper, bronze, gold, and silver were worked. Their usual supplies came from tribes on the borders of the empire, who had considerable quantities of metal and who were, moreover, easy victims; but some Guarani raiding parties, driven by their greed, would cross the Inca boundary and risk expeditions into the interior of the empire. The Spanish chroniclers, who collected the historical traditions of old Peru, often mention these raids and recount how the emperors Yupanqui and Huayna Capac fortified their frontiers to stop the "barbarians." The ruins that remain to this day enable us to reconstruct what these defense works were like. With the passage of time Guarani Indians increased their pressure on the Inca advance posts and in the end occupied the territory they had conquered. Their descendants, the Chiriguano Indians, speak Guarani and have not forgotten their old home, Paraguay, as they showed at the time of the 1934 war between that country and Bolivia.

The Guarani raiders coveted above all the axes and knives in copper and bronze, much better tools than those in stone and bone they were accustomed to using. However, they did not disdain metal ornaments. A few examples of these reached the coastal people in the Río de la Plata by successive trading exchanges. This is why the Portuguese and Spaniards found bracelets and breastplates in gold and silver among relatively primitive Indians, ignorant of how to extract or work those metals. Asked about the origin of such pieces, they would point to the setting sun, talk vaguely about "a mountain of silver," of a white king,

6

huts built of stone, and domesticated "long-haired deer"—the llamas.

The stories told about this distant and mysterious land, at least as much as could be understood of them, led some members of the Solis expedition, wrecked at Santa Catarina, to set off for that far country about which their hosts, the Cario Indians, never tired of talking. Five of them, led by the Portuguese Alejo Garcia, went overland to Paraguay, where they joined a band of Guarani warriors and razed several Peruvian villages. Alejo Garcia returned to Paraguay, followed, it is said, by a troop of prisoners carrying rich booty. He was killed by some Tupi Indians before he got back to the Santa Catarina region where his companions were awaiting him, but some of his captives succeeded in reaching the coast with a little gold and silver. When, in their turn, the conquistadores reached Paraguay, eager to follow the exploits of Alejo Garcia, the Guaranis gave them much information about this bold adventurer who, some dozen years before Pizarro, was the first white man to penetrate the Inca empire.

The "joyfull newes" of the "mountain of silver" and of the white king was not slow to cross the oceans. Although the Inca empire was as yet unexplored, stories of its unparalleled wealth and the fascination it had for the savage tribes drew ships as if by a magnet to the shores of the Pacific and the Atlantic.

In 1526, a fleet commanded by Sebastian Cabot left Spain for the Moluccas. Profits from the spice trade were substantial, but a more alluring prospect beckoned. Like so many others, Cabot had heard the stories of a mysterious land of great wealth. Consequently, without hesitation, he changed his course and sailed westward toward the River Plate. If he had had any doubts about the wisdom of his project, they were soon dispelled by the shipwrecked sailors of Santa Catarina, who told him the story of Alejo Garcia and assured him that

if he went up the River Plate it would be easy to load his ships with gold and silver, even if they were bigger than they were, for the Parana river, and the tributaries that fell into it, led to a mountain to which the Indians were accustomed to travel, and in that mountain there were various kinds of metal and much gold and silver and another metal they did not know [no doubt bronze].

7

Working gold in the Peruvian mines (Bry)

They also told him that "they knew from hearsay that the inhabitants of that mountain had silver crowns on their heads and plates of gold around their necks." They even showed him samples of this gold.

Cabot acted on this information. He followed the "Río de la Plata" (the River Plate) upstream and then along the Paraná to Paraguay. The Guarani Indians he found there were well provided with silver ornaments and even some of gold, but the booty was as nothing compared to the abundant and precise information he gathered about the "masters of metal." But the plains of bush that seemed to stretch into infinity lay in between. Living under miserable conditions and surrounded by hostile tribes, the Spaniards were reduced to living on rats and dogs, but their miseries were forgotten as they listened to the wonderful tales the Indians told them of the "mountain of silver and the white king." Sebastian Cabot's expedition was a total failure. It has left only one mark on history, a proper noun, the memory of a dream, the Río de la Plata, "the Silver River," so called because it was believed that its muddy waters led to the wonderful mountain.

While Cabot was trying to reach Peru by the great rivers of the Argentine pampas, Pizarro and Almagro were also approaching this rich land by following the Pacific coast southward. The days of the Inca empire, threatened from two sides, were numbered.

In 1535 the biggest army Spain had ever sent to the West Indies embarked in a fleet "worthy of Caesar." Its commander, the very noble Adelantado Pedro de Mendoza, was pleased to believe that he would succeed where Cabot had failed. Actually, at the time of his departure from Spain the Inca empire was already in Spanish hands. The treasure of Atahuallpa's ransom had reached Seville six months earlier. Strange as it may seem, nobody in Mendoza's huge expedition seems to have been told that the "mountain of silver" which he wished to conquer was none other than that Peru whose emperor, the "white king" of the story, had been strangled two years previously. Mendoza and his companions were pursuing a will o' the wisp, an empire that had ceased to exist.

We will not elaborate on this disastrous expedition. In 1540, Ayola, one of Pedro de Mendoza's lieutenants, reached the "silver mountain," that is to say the cordillera of the Andes, but he and all his band were massacred on their return. In 1548, Irala, chasing the same phantom, left Paraguay and in his turn reached the borders of Peru. His countrymen already settled there viewed this intruder from the Atlantic with a resentment that made him retrace his steps, but he still clung to the hope of conquering some other and still richer empire. Such were the Spaniards' powers of self-deception that the search for a fabulous country, where gold and silver were as common as pebbles, persisted for more than a century and it never occurred to them that they were looking for a kingdom they had already conquered. The Indians had indeed described the place in terms which should have opened the eyes of the most naive, going so far as to point out its actual position toward the setting sun, to the west, but the conquistadores obstinately placed it somewhere to the east of the Andes, to the north of Paraguay or in eastern Bolivia.

10

Neither the sufferings of the members of these expeditions nor the futility of their efforts could weaken the Spaniards' faith in the eventual discovery of this Eldorado. It was not until much later, when the Jesuits had undertaken the spiritual conquest of Amazonia, that the dream faded away. Each of these foolish "entries" cost blood. To the Spaniards who died, lost in the forests, must be added the hundreds or thousands of Indians who perished from exhaustion or were massacred. All that is left to show for all the effort and the disappointed expectations is a few records in the archives and the names of some extinct tribes. These chimeras have also left a slight trace in French literature. Candide and his servant Cacambo, who "spoke Peruvian," after fleeing from Paraguay reached Eldorado, where they learned from an old man that they were in "the ancient country of the Incas," a country which had been able to keep its riches and its customs intact. Voltaire drew on the Jesuit historians of Paraguay for his chapter on Eldorado, the country the Spaniards searched for in vain, not far from the area where the order founded its famous missions.

In South America the myth of the Amazons, common to both the Old and the New World, was reinforced by a more or less imaginary vision of the Inca empire. The kingdom of women without men was mistaken for Peru, or placed in its neighborhood. The Dominican monk Gaspar de Carvajal, who took part in the first expedition up the Amazon, in the company of Orellana (1541), and was its historian, says he was blinded in fighting these formidable warriors. This skirmish has been immortalized by the name of the huge American river; it took place a little before Orellana reached its mouth. Before meeting the Amazons Carvajal had heard that they were very rich and that they drew a tribute of feathers and parrots from subject tribes. He said he got all his information from an Indian, using a vocabulary he himself had made. In this way he established that the kingdom of the Amazons consisted of "seventy *pueblos* built in stone with town gates, joined by roads and protected by walls and guard posts." His informant also told him that "among these women there was a lady who reigned over all the rest, that the country was very rich in gold and silver and that only the lower classes used wooden vessels, except those used for cooking, which were of clay." Finally, he said that

in the capital and main town, where this lady lived, there were five very big buildings, which were holy and consecrated to the Sun . . . and in these were many idols in gold and silver in female form, and gold and silver vessels for the worship of the Sun, and that the women were all dressed in very fine-spun woolen cloth, for in that country there were numerous sheep, like those in Peru.

A few years later, the Spaniards who were with Alvar Nuñez Cabeza de Vaca in his unfortunate expedition collected another version of the Amazon myth from the Indians of upper Paraguay, who maintained that a short distance away there were warrior women who had great treasure and ate from a gold and silver service. They even added the following details: in the neighborhood of these women there were some big towns and a lake called "House of the Sun" where that star was kept; the natives of the country wore clothes, lived in huts made of stone, used long-haired deer, and had built such a big town that it could not be crossed in a single day. These allusions to Peru became yet clearer when the Indians stated that on the other side of the mountains there was a great stretch of water and that the Spaniards there went about on horseback.

It has been suggested that the myth of the Amazons arose from a confused knowledge of the Inca institution of the *acllacuna,* or chosen women, enclosed in a kind of convent. The legendary theme of women without men was no doubt known to the forest Indians well before the advent of the Inca empire. If it owed something to the prestige of this great kingdom, it was merely a few additional details, such as the wealth of precious metals, the stone buildings, and the power of these fabulous beings. As with the Eldorado of the Spaniards, the forest Indians' country of the Amazons was endowed with all the real and imaginary marvels attributed by them to the mysterious land that lay toward the sunset.

The discovery and quick, brutal conquest of the Inca kingdom greatly impressed Europe. From 1534 onward written reports, forerunners of our newspapers, circulated in Italy, Germany, and France, describing Peru, its wealth, and the fantastic ransom paid to Pizarro by the emperor Atahuallpa. These pamphlets reproduced more or less accurately the content of letters or reports

The tragedy at Cajamarca (Bry)

The taking of Cuzco (Bry)

sent from Panama by the officers of the Crown to the King of Spain. A broadsheet printed at Lyons in 1534, with the title *Nouvelles certaines des isles du Pérou*, promises its readers "Many new things, so much inestimable wealth of gold and silver and precious stones found in that province and brought here from that country." In fact this publication contains an account of the capture of Atahuallpa and some details about Peruvian roads and suspension bridges. It ends by describing the principal pieces of treasure the Inca gave to Pizarro as his ransom, much of which had been sent to the King of Spain.

An Italian report appearing about the same time departed further from the truth. It showed its readers the emperor of Peru carried in his golden litter encrusted with precious stones. According to the author of this report all the goods of the earth had been lavished on Peru, since, in addition to his fabulous ransom, Atahuallpa had added a thousand loads of cinnamon. Peru was well described as "God's vineyard."

When he read Gomara, Montaigne was much moved by the fate of the Inca. In his chapter "Des coches" he departs from his usual philosophic detachment and becomes indignant at the gratuitous cruelty of the Spaniards, to whom he denies any glory for a too easy victory. He denounces Pizarro for his bad faith in executing Atahuallpa, who had given "in his discourse signs of a liberal and steadfast courage and of a clear, reasonable mind" and had, above all, faithfully paid his ransom. He admired what he knew of Peruvian civilization. Of the great Inca roads he says, "Neither Greece, nor Rome, nor Egypt can show anything to compare in usefulness, difficulties overcome or nobility with these works." The excellence of the Indians was shown not only in their industries. They were superior to us also on the moral plane. And in devotion to duty, observance of the law, liberality, loyalty, and sincerity, it is clear that we are inferior to them: by these very advantages they were betrayed and lost.

If the mineral resources of the Incas gave rise to the legend of the Eldorado, their institutions, as described by the Spaniards, started another legend: that of a utopia, one which was a perfect and ideal socialist state, one created before the word was coined.

It was during the eighteenth century above all that philosophers, novelists, and dramatists delighted in presenting the picture of a Peruvian empire whose rulers, full of virtue, secured the happiness of their simple people by their wise laws. We cannot be sure that Campanella was thinking of Peru when writing his *City of the Sun;* on the other hand Morelly, a precursor of socialism, tells us in the preface to his *Basiliade* (1753)—a kind of philosophic epic—

that the whole plot of his poem proves the possibility of a system which is not in the least imaginary, for the people governed by Zeinzeminn resemble very closely the people of the most flourishing and best governed Empire the world has ever known; I mean that of the Peruvians. (*The shipwreck of the floating islands or the Basiliade of the celebrated Pilpai, an epic poem translated from the Indian by Mr. M. . . . .,* 1753.)

The Inca empire presented the Abbé Raynal with a difficult problem: how to reconcile, on the one hand, his conviction that only private property could bring about prosperity and raise nations to greatness and, on the other, the fact that the Peruvians

The noble savage: from the *History of the Incas,* Garcilaso de la Vega

were fully prosperous under a collectivist system. He explains with embarrassment that, if their system has not led to depopulation and anarchy, "it is because the Incas had no knowledge of a tax system and, since they had to provide for the needs of government from natural resources alone, were impelled to seek the increase of these resources." He completed his case by the strange argument that "the wealth and well-being of the Inca is so closely allied to that of his subjects that it is not possible to fertilize one without fertilizing the other." The eighteenth century believed in the perfection of the Inca state, some because they thought it communist and others because it was subject to an enlightened despotism.

Marmontel's novel *The Incas,* insipid and boring though it may be to our eyes, was once widely read, for, at a time when the world was bewitched by the idea of the noble savage, it showed a people whom laws had made perfect:

All their customs had been codified as laws: these laws like those of Athens punished idleness and laziness; but in insisting on work they removed poverty; and man, forced to become useful, could at least hope to be happy. The laws protected modesty as something inviolable and holy; liberty as the most sacred thing in nature; innocence, honor, and domestic peace as the gifts of heaven that must be revered.

Among the Incas even the theocracy, so hated by Marmontel, was appealing, for "the habit of good behavior made laws unnecessary: they were deterrent in nature, not vengeful."

The enthusiasm aroused by the institutions of the Incas in the "Age of Reason" in Europe had declined by the time the bourgeoisie triumphed. The great social movements of our age, however, should revive interest in the image of a partially socialist Inca empire.

No one has better expressed this view than the Peruvian ethnographer and historian Luis Valcárcel. According to him the genius of the Incas showed itself above all in their management of economic affairs. "All our historical sources," he said, "confirm that there have been few, if any, civilizations as well organized for the conservation and expansion of man's existence."

The state, great and sole entrepreneur, having statistical and administrative services at its disposal as well as laws, precepts, discipline, and a dynamic creative urge, was able to mobilize the whole population and do away with unproductive unemployment and parasitism: it abolished the distinction between economic, political, and technical activities. An analysis of this phenomenon shows us the socialist nature of Tahuantin-suyu. It is the Peruvian brand of socialism.

Like so many others before me, I am trying to describe the strange Inca civilization, to which Toynbee gave a leading place

17

in his list of twenty-one original civilizations. The great development of ethnology allows us today to re-examine the familiar evidence in a new light. In the last twenty years archaeology has upset all our ideas about the origin and evolution of Peruvian cultures. Furthermore, it has too often been forgotten that the descendants of the Incas are still to be found in considerable numbers: a population of six or seven million makes up the biggest and most compact indigenous group in the Americas. Although over four centuries their customs, beliefs, and institutions have greatly changed, it is still possible to fill in the gaps in the written records from the evidence still discernible in the vestiges of the ancient order. Study of administrative records is often more fruitful than an elaborate examination of the classic works on the Inca empire. Progress in social anthropology, by turning us away from our ethnocentricity, has allowed a better interpretation of customs and traditions that hitherto have been shown to us only through Western eyes. Such research has in no way decreased the admiration the Inca empire merits; on the contrary it has brought to light the true originality of its institutions and the difficulties it overcame in establishing such a vast and prosperous state.

The word "Inca" as currently used is ambiguous and its meaning has been altered from the original one—chief. The sovereign of Peru was, *par excellence,* the Inca, a title also given to members of his family and branches related to it. The term was even extended to include the allied groups of people from whom the imperial civil servants were recruited. The word Inca, then, could be translated as sovereign or nobleman.

Today the word, both as noun and adjective, is used for everything having to do with the history or the civilization of the Inca dynasty. It is particularly applied to the people over whom the Inca reigned. One might, in all logic, apply it equally well to the modern Indians of the Andean region of Ecuador, Peru, and Bolivia, who, to a great extent, are the direct heirs of the civilization that flourished under the rulers bearing that name. During the colonial period only nobles of imperial descent had the right to the title of Inca, the term having not yet lost its true meaning.

The missionaries gave the name of Quechua to the *runa-simi,*

18

or language of men, and it is by the former name that the Indians who speak it are known to this day. Once again chance and confusion have decided the destiny of a word, because quechua really means the agricultural land in the Andes valleys between 3,000 and 11,000 feet above sea level. It was in this favored region that there arose this people who, under the Inca dynasty, were to found a mighty empire. The history of the Indians of Peru falls then into two periods: that of the Incas proper, which ended in the sixteenth century, and that of the Quechuas, which exists to this day and will continue until the Indians of the three Andean republics have finally been integrated with the population of Spanish origin.

The Precursors

When in the thirteenth or fourteenth century of our era a small mountain tribe penetrated the Cuzco valley, which lies some 11,000 feet above sea level, and founded the greatest pre-Columbian American empire, more than ten cultures had already been developed there in the highlands and deserts stretching from Ecuador to Bolivia. The conquering Incas, latecomers on the Andean scene, inherited a tradition some four thousand years old. In the last century every Peruvian or Bolivian ruin, and every piece of pottery or cloth obtained from the looting pillage of the huge graveyards on the coast, was indiscriminately ascribed to the Incas. Historical sources give the Incas a duration of only a few centuries, making the Andean civilizations seem without depth. To attribute their origin to about the period of the foundation of the Christian era appeared almost audacious. To explain this rapid flowering of a civilization of such undeniable brilliance, people were pleased to imagine all sorts of outside influences from across the seas. Egypt, India, Cambodia, China, and Polynesia have all, in turn, been invoked to explain some aspect of

Sechin sculpture, Chavin period: the wounded warrior

art or architecture, or even an institution, whose parallel could be found in the Old World.

A half-century of patient excavation, of which the great German archaeologist Max Uhle was the pioneer, has modified this summary view of the origin of the Andean cultures. We now know that nine thousand years ago men scarcely different from the modern Indian were moving about the Andean valleys, on the high plateaus, and on the shores of the Pacific, as small bands of hunters. Some of their tools have been recovered in rock shelters or picked out of the soil on old encampment sites. The skeleton of such a man was discovered in a cave at Lauricocha in 1965. The great heaps of shells, the remains of numerous meals, scattered along the Pacific coast, testify to the antiquity of human occupation in these desolate regions. These deserts, among the most arid on earth, were populated from the third millennium B.C. by an unknown people living in underground houses. These are found along the banks of rivers which, cutting through the sands, bring life and prosperity to their valleys. These people, in addition to fishing, practiced a little rudimentary agriculture. The Humboldt Current, running along the Peruvian coast, may be likened to a huge river whose cold waters, full of plankton, are among the richest fishing areas of the world. However inhospitable the area might be, man there was assured of abundant food. He shared it with the millions of birds that frequented this coast.

These coastal peoples had made considerable technical progress: gathered into villages, they had a varied collection of tools and, although they had no loom, made cloth by an ingenious method. Neither the advent of pottery, which appeared about 1200 B.C., nor progress in agriculture and crafts made much difference to the life of these archaic people during the course of this initial period (1200 B.C. to 700 B.C.); they continued their slow development in the coastal valleys.

Toward the end of the eighth century B.C., maize, up to then unknown, began to be used for food. Where did this wonderful cereal come from? A cereal which the Indians, fully alive to its vital role in their economy, personified as a "sister" and "mother." In spite of intensive research by botanists we still do not know from what part of America it arose, no doubt after a long period of hybridization. Recent discoveries of fossil pollen favor the view that it originated in Central America. Be that as it may, it was from the north that this plant seems to have come to Peru.

The growing of maize coincided with a sudden change in the cultural evolution of the Andean area. A complex and vigorous civilization manifests itself by an architectural and artistic style in central and northern Peru, both in the mountains and along the coast. The Chavin site, in an Andean valley to the north of Lima, has given its name to this archaeological "horizon"; it is famous for the huge ruins of a sanctuary, consisting of massive platforms pierced with galleries, and rooms one above the other.

The diffusion of this art form does not imply, as was once believed, that there was a huge empire which took in a great part of modern Peru. Chavin might well have been either the capital of a small theocratic state drawing its labor from neighboring agricultural peoples, or possibly a pilgrimage center frequented by millions of the faithful, as was the temple of Pachacamac to the south of Lima during the Inca period, and as is today the sanctuary of Copacabana on Lake Titicaca, now visited on the average by sixty thousand Indians a year. It was perhaps with the help of such Indian pilgrims that the temple of Chavin was built, and there is no doubt that its prestige led to the diffusion of this artistic style. Whatever hypothesis we adopt it is nonetheless certain that Chavin was the first great Peruvian civilization whose influence extended over a vast area. There was nothing comparable until the Tiahuanaco civilization (tenth century A.D.) and the Inca (fourteenth century A.D.).

It is from the Chavin period that we first trace the crystallization of those characteristics of the Andean cultures which, to us, are above all represented by the Inca civilization. The growth of maize and several other new plants had added to the resources of a population tending more and more to concentrate in straggling villages. Architecture, particularly religious architecture, reached an advanced state of development and builders used worked stone. Sculpture produced some masterpieces, though the artists, limited by their material, excelled in bas-relief rather than work in the round. The development of cloth was advanced by the discovery or adoption of the loom.

The Chavin horizon pottery, best known from the excavations

24

at Cupisnique, foreshadowed the richness and variety of the Mochica pottery in the north. Almost the only metal worked was gold, and admirable specimens have been obtained from tombs. Behind these massive buildings and this artistic and technical achievement the outline of an organized state can be felt, no doubt under the authority of a priestly caste. It is during this period that the great cosmic myths and political institutions arose, to be inherited by the Incas eighteen centuries later.

Excavation shows us that in the second or third century A.D. the Chavin period was succeeded by the first intermediate epoch, called the "Experimenter" because of the new techniques being used in agriculture, architecture, and pottery. This period, in contrast to its predecessor, lacks unity. There is but a chronological link to group the various local cultures flourishing at this period, both on the coast and in the mountains: such cultures are the Gallinazo, Salinar, Paracas, Chanapata (near Cuzco), and Chirapa in Bolivia.

The "Experimenter" is the initial phase of the civilizations known as "Classic." In effect, while the Chavin style disappeared rather suddenly from the huge area it at one time covered, the "Experimenter" period cultures show no break in continuity. The transition from one to the other was imperceptible.

The Classic age of Peruvian archaeology corresponds with the period known as that of the "Master Craftsmen," or simply the "Flowering." A few years ago it was placed in the period between the sixth and tenth centuries A.D. Today the experts place the extreme limits of the period between the third century B.C. and the tenth century A.D. However that may be, it is admitted that toward the beginning of our Christian era the numerous local civilizations, whose constant progress has been demonstrated by archaeologists, attained their full maturity in the north of Peru, in the Moche, Chicama, and Viru valleys, and in the south in the Nazca region. Town life was organized within the framework of a true state. Arts and crafts were at their height.

The north-coast Indians, to whom the name of Mochica has been given, or sometimes Proto-Chimu to distinguish them from their heirs, the Chimu, are only known to us by the contents of their graves, wonderfully preserved by the sand, and above all by the realistic style of their art. Ironically, as often happens in

Mochica culture: warrior demon

archaeology, their daily life, as well as certain elements of their mythology, is known to us, while their language, their history, their beliefs, and their customs are not.

The thousands of pots excavated from Mochica tombs (the Larco Herrera Museum at Lima alone has more than 50,000 of them) by their modeling and painting bring to life a complex and refined society. The Mochica potters sought to portray their contemporaries with unusual realism and accuracy. Their choice was eclectic; there was no class nor condition which would not do as a model. Beauty and ugliness were equally inspiring. Finally, they were as interested in portraying the miserable side of existence as the noble, the erotic as the supernatural. Certain things shown in their pottery forecast scenes actually witnessed by the Spaniards when they entered the Inca empire. The Mochica sovereigns, crowned with a diadem and covered with jewels, are sitting in a litter, just as was Atahuallpa when he appeared in the great square of Cajamarca on November 16, 1532. A few days later the conquistadores, having captured the Inca emperor, were astonished to see that not one of his subjects, great dignitary or simple servant, approached him without a burden on his back symbolic of humility. So, on the Mochica pottery, small people, moving toward someone whose height shows him to be a ruler, are bowed beneath the weight of a symbolic burden.

If we leave aside these traces of a court ceremonial whose tradition reaches back to the beginning of our era and turn to other subjects, we find many parallels between Mochica and Inca in spite of the thousand years separating them. In the Mochica soldiers, painted on the sides of pots or modeled in the round, we can see the Inca troops that faced the Spaniards on the road to Cuzco. Their equipment is much the same: sling, spear thrower, stone- or metal-headed club, helmet, and square shield. It would not be too much of an anachronism to illustrate the military might of the Incas from Mochica pottery.

Many of the less spectacular aspects of Mochica culture as shown by its potters have their equivalents in the sixteenth-century Spanish texts describing the daily life of the Incas: cloth workshops where the women made admirable stuffs on primitive looms, surgical operations, the arrival of messengers, games, religious ceremonies. On one of the big polychrome frescoes on a Mochica pyramid one can still distinguish a scene of certain anthropomorphic artifacts in revolt against their owners. It is an old story, common to both Mayas and Incas, one version of which was found in the seventeenth century and another a few years ago, among Chiriguano and Tacana Indians living on the borders of the Inca empire. Thus many Mochica beliefs were

Mochica culture: Pyramid of the Sun

shared by the Incas.

The wealth of the Mochica state, attested by the richness of funeral goods in the graves, rested on a well-planned agriculture. A gigantic network of canals used the waters of the coastal rivers to fertilize great stretches of sand. The remains of this giant irrigation system are among the most surprising things in pre-Columbian America. For instance, the great Ascope aqueduct was about fifty feet high in places and crossed a valley nearly a mile in width. In the Chicama valley the traces of a deep canal can be followed for more than seventy-five miles.

Works on this scale imply a series of decisions taken by a central authority sufficiently powerful to raise and direct the numerous gangs needed to carry out such enterprises. The use of the water, the maintenance of the canals and aqueducts, the repair of sluices would only be possible under the control of an effective government. The conquest of the Peruvian coastal desert postulates the existence of a respected central authority and a well-organized civil service, as in ancient Egypt and Mesopotamia. Karl Marx has indicated the role of irrigation in the formation of despotic governments of the Asiatic type. More recently a German sociologist, Karl A. Wittfogel, has tried to explain the struggle for the control of water as the characteristic of certain civilizations to which he has given the name of "hydraulic," in contrast to those he calls "feudal."

In any case Wittfogel's interpretation is valid for the pre-Incaic civilizations of the Pacific coast. Certain scenes depicted on Mochica pottery leave no doubt as to the semidivine nature of their chiefs and the superstitious respect with which they were surrounded. Apart from these the pyramids of the Sun and Moon at Moche bear witness to the extent of the power of these sovereigns who, in their cases, were veritable little pharaohs. The political system created by the Mochica despots, together with the civil service, outlived their period and were adopted by their successors. The Chimu kingdom, which replaced that of the Mochica between the tenth and fifteenth centuries of our era, was in many respects their heir. Just as Chimu art, in spite of its monotony and lack of vigor, was directly related to that of the old Mochica, so the Chimu state kept intact until the arrival of the Spaniards the political and administrative system that had been inherited, in outline, from its precursors. The Incas, originally a fairly crude mountain people, came strongly under the cultural influence of the Chimu kingdom. We know that the Inca Tupac Yupanqui moved a number of Chimu potters to the capital, thus renewing the potter's art in the heart of his kingdom. However, the influence of these old coastal civilizations was not limited to arts and crafts. Inca court ceremonial was based on that in use among the Chimu princes. It is very probable that the administrative system of the Incas had also been borrowed from the Chimus, who in their turn had it from the Mochicas. On the other hand the almost contemporary Nazca culture plays no part in the relationship we are trying to establish between the old civilization of Peru and that of the Incas.

Archaeologists give the name "Expansionist" to the period following the classic Mochica and Nazca cultures. This was the period of the Tiahuanaco civilization, whose highest point of development is seen in the village of that name to the south of Lake Titicaca. There, at an altitude of 13,000 feet, on a cold and wind-swept plain, one finds scattered over the ground a collection of megalithic monuments that are among the most imposing of pre-Columbian America. They were already in ruins when the Incas took over the region in the fifteenth century, inhabited then, as now, by Aymara Indians. The Incas were as ignorant of the origin and history of this extinct town as we are. No doubt they believed it to be very ancient, for it is at Tiahuanaco that the supreme god Viracocha is supposed to have created men after statues he had already carved in stone. We can be sure it was the huge, stiff, ugly statues which stood among the rubble of Tiahuanaco, in greater numbers than today, that inspired this ancient Andean myth.

Without an oral tradition to guide us, we still wonder how a people living in a region as inhospitable as the Bolivian puna could move such huge blocks of sandstone or basalt, weighing up to a hundred tons each, even if the quarries used were not as far away as has been supposed. Although the builders of Tiahuanaco knew the use of copper tools, making scissors and holding-cramps from it, the art with which these immense blocks were cut, polished, and embellished with niches and bas-reliefs still fills one with wonder. One is amazed at the boldness and patience of these men, who often constructed their works with mortise and tenon as if they were carpenters. The Tiahuanaco ruins have given rise to all sorts of ridiculous theories. One such theory attributes a tremendous antiquity to the ruins on the basis of so-called astronomical observations. Thirty years ago Tiahuanaco was being described even in serious books as the capital of a "megalithic empire," almost equal to that of the Incas in size and greater in power and artistic achievement. The builders of Tiahuanaco having been identified as Aymara Indians, attempts were made to prove by onomatology that their language had been in use from Argentina to Peru.

The theory of a great Tiahuanaco empire preceding that of the

Llama, Tiahuanaco period

Incas has not survived our greater modern knowledge of the Andean past, a knowledge gained by systematic excavation. It is quite possible, even probable, that the spread of the Tiahuanaco culture was the result of military pressure by two or three states whose existence can only be surmised. Nevertheless trade and especially the power and prestige exercised by a religious center are

Giant statue, Tiahuanaco

sufficient to explain the use of these art forms in the mountains and on the coast. Even Tiahuanaco has been deprived of its fame as a great American metropolis and is instead regarded simply as a holy city, most of its buildings having a religious significance. One exception is the Akapana hill which, with its water reservoir and walled slopes, may have been a fortress. Many of these problems could be solved if one could prove the archaeologist W. C. Bennett's conjecture that Tiahuanaco was built little by little, with the sporadic help of thousands of pilgrims. Many of the buildings appear unfinished; even the famous Gate of the Sun itself does not seem to have been put in its proper place and some of the bas-reliefs that adorn it have not received their final touches.

Archaeologists consider the Tiahuanaco period to have been a particularly troubled one, though possibly they base this view on somewhat slender evidence. The more highly populated nations of the Classic period were constantly at war with each other; wars that led either to mutual destruction or to union. Even if one admits that the Tiahuanaco culture was the work of a conquering nation, it does not appear that they had anticipated the Incas in being able to organize and administer their conquered lands. On the coast there is no town, no monument, that can assuredly be attributed to them. It is only by the grave goods that we can assume the predominance of a new art coming from the highlands.

Among the coastal peoples the Tiahuanaco style becomes simplified and dull, and for this reason it and the period in which it is found have been described as "epigonal." Today the name Huari-Tiahuanaco is used, for, near Huari, in the Mantaro valley, a style of architecture and pottery has been found which shows Tiahuanaco influence in many respects. Huari thus seems to be the source of the provincial style of Tiahuanaco art used in the coastal cultures.

The Huari civilization had its center in a region bordering the area where the Inca nation developed. Huari influence was sufficiently strong to modify their neighbors' local traditions, and to introduce in their pottery a style from which, after a long development, the Inca decorative arts were to spring. Archaeologists assure us that inventories of excavations and topographical surveys give irrefutable proof of a political and social change during the Ex-

Wooden idol (Huaca del Dragon)

Ruins of Chanchan (Chimu)

pansionist period. Governments which in the Classic age were strongly theocratic (the total of effort put into the building of temples proves it) became military. The soldier took the place of the priest, a result of the wars that divided each of these little states from its neighbors. This secularization of life is shown by the increase in number and importance of civil buildings and, a new phenomenon, the building of large towns to a fixed and regular pattern. To this day one can easily distinguish the aristocratic or administrative quarters from the homes of the common people; the former are decorated and spacious while the latter consist of lightly built houses enclosed within a high-walled rectangle. The ruins of Chanchan, a few miles from the modern town of Trujillo, though they have been exposed to much disgraceful vandalism, still cover an area of about six and a half square miles. The old capital of the Chimus was divided into quarters, each surrounded by massive walls. The open land was used for cisterns, canals, vegetable gardens, and cemeteries.

The strange arrangement of this, the largest city of the New World before the arrival of Columbus, clearly shows the Chimu social system. Each block belongs to a clan or line (*ayllu*). Many things characteristic of the urban Chimu can be found in the Inca cities, another proof of the influence exercised by the civilized people of the coast over their mountain neighbors.

The founding and growth of cities are two phenomena so characteristic of the centuries that preceded the conquest that one easily accepts the name of "City Builder" proposed for this period. With the City Builders we enter the true historical era. The principal states existing during this period were subjugated by the Incas during the second half of the fifteenth century. At the time of the arrival of the Spaniards, though politically these states were part of the empire, they nevertheless kept their own languages, customs, and government. The best known of these states was the Chimu, centered on the Moche valley but dominating the whole of the north of Peru from the region of Lambayeque, or even of Tumbez, to Lima. Its language was still spoken up to a fews years ago in the village of Eten, near Chiclayo.

The Chimus, like the Mochica, made irrigation their greatest concern. Their livelihood was so closely tied to the water supply that the Inca Yupanqui had only to threaten to cut their canals for them to submit and be incorporated in the Inca empire. Grave goods suggest that society was rigidly divided into social strata, and this is confirmed by historical documents. The heavy bastions of the Paramonga fortress and the ruins of the garrison towns protecting the irrigation canals show the preoccupations of this civilization whose wealth exposed it to the cupidity and hate of its neighbors.

The rapid development of a working class is explained by the social hierarchy and the considerable division of labor. For example, pottery was mass-produced by molds and thus lost much of its originality and vigor. Cotton cloth was made in considerable quantity in veritable workshops. This bulk production, almost an industrial one, was naturally accompanied by the standardiza-

36

tion of taste which characterizes the Inca culture.

This period is of particular interest to us because it corresponds more or less with the birth of the Inca empire, the remote origins of which archaeology has done little to uncover up to now. The oldest culture known in the Cuzco valley is Chanapata—a site discovered on the Carmenca hill just outside the town. The American archaeologist John H. Rowe found there the foundation of a thick wall and several round or oval tombs containing skeletons but no grave goods. The potsherds discovered here were decorated with purely geometric color designs, painted, incised, or polished. The Chanapata pottery somewhat recalls that of Chavin, but is more like the Chirapa, a site dated as being before the Tiahuanaco period. Nevertheless, in spite of these resemblances, Chanapata cannot be placed accurately among the periods indicated above. One thing is certain: there is a hiatus between this archaic culture and that of the Incas, which dates from around the year A.D. 1200. So far nothing has been found to fill this gap in our knowledge.

The fortress of Sacsahuamán and the K'illke site provide the oldest Inca pottery, and it makes a poor showing beside the Tiahuanaco work by which Inca art was inspired. It consists of ill-made pieces with only polychrome geometric patterns, and the classic (or "Imperial Cuzco") Inca ceramics are derived from it. In spite of a banality naturally inherent in mass-produced articles, the pottery of this period shows some development as time goes on.

Inca pottery with its "aryballus," duck-billed plates and beakers, is easily identified. As its age is known (fourteenth to fifteenth century A.D.), archaeologists use it to a great extent for the purposes of dating. Numerous pieces are found anywhere the Inca armies have been or along their *limes*. Much of this material comes from the neighborhood of ruins of buildings recognizable as Inca from their style or from oral tradition.

The Thirteen Emperors

Who were the Incas? Where did they come from? When the Spaniards asked these questions, either from curiosity or from some legal scruple, the Indians answered with long quasi-historical and semilegendary accounts. Perhaps now is the time to question the historical value of the often very detailed traditions recorded by the Spanish chroniclers, who say they obtained them from very reliable informants. Among these people many seem to have been chosen with care: princes of the imperial blood, professional chroniclers, learned men qualified by age and experience. Many of the accounts collected by the colonial civil servants came from the *quipu-kamayoc,* or the masters of the knotted cords, the famous *quipus* used by specialists to keep the government accounts. Did these cords serve as writing? Were the scribes able to record the notable events of each reign? Some of the chroniclers state that this is the case, though the evidence is weak. It seems highly improbable that the shape of a knot and its position on a series of cords could have any meaning other than an arithmetical one. These so-called royal annals may have been

Map of the Inca empire

no more than numerical accounts dealing with the length of a reign, tribute collected, gangs employed in the building of some palace, or simply a population census or summary of the armed forces available.

The lives of the Incas and their exploits were preserved in songs and ballads and no doubt much embellished. They were sung or chanted at certain feasts, but principally at Inca funerals. The mummies of all the Inca's predecessors were brought out into the big square in Cuzco and the priests or bards attached to each Inca chanted, in turn, a eulogy of his deified emperor. This ceremony ended with the recitation of the great deeds of the newly deceased emperor. Witnesses to the existence of these heroic poems, which kept alive the virtues and exploits of the Incas, are too numerous and too exact to be doubted, even if the evidence is not conclusive enough to support the view that they resembled the Spanish *romances* and *villancicos,* as the chroniclers maintained. Whatever may be said, they were not epic poems properly speaking, but relatively short, easily remembered ballads. No doubt there were a great many for each emperor and they formed a series. The rhythm and movement of these poems, and even certain devices that could be called "literary," can sometimes be traced in the histories of the Incas written by men like Betanzos and Sarmiento, whose informants derived their historical knowledge from ballads themselves. Pachacuti's war against the Chancas, his accession to the throne in spite of his father's opposition, his eventual triumph, all more or less historical events, are presented like the episodes in a medieval verse chronicle. The accounts of other reigns similarly contain anecdotes in which one catches echoes of poems now forever lost.

The *harawi,* songs celebrating the power and conquests of the Incas, were heard for the last time in Cuzco in 1616. The Jesuits wanted to celebrate the beatification of Saint Ignacio with great ceremony, and this served as an excuse for some thirty thousand descendants of the Incas to revive the ceremonies and feasts of the extinct empire. In order not to alarm the Spaniards, all the parades, dances, mock battles, and ceremonial marches of the imperial guards were made under the aegis of the Infant Jesus "dressed as Inca."

A tradition recorded by Sarmiento says that the Inca Pachacuti used to summon all the provincial "historians" to his capital, and after considerable questioning a painting would be made on some boards of the more remarkable events they had told. These "historical pictures" were put into a hall of the Temple of the Sun where only the emperor and accredited chroniclers were allowed. Scenes of battle, hunting, and court life that are shown on the lacquered beakers (*querus*) of the colonial period, some dating from the Inca epoch, indicate that the Incas did have sufficient artistic tradition and technical knowledge to make the existence of such records possible, but the majority of our ancient sources of information are silent on the subject. There is no other evidence that the Incas had pictographic records, as did the Aztecs.

Most of the chroniclers agree as to the names and the order of succession of the thirteen emperors of the Inca dynasty. At first sight the precision with which their reigns are numbered, and the stories they tell us, inspire confidence. We draw the conclusion that here we have a strong historical tradition, handing down the story intact over several centuries. On closer examination this favorable impression is found to be illusory. Behind a superabundance of often insignificant detail the big historical events grow blurred and, in spite of their apparent exactitude, are found to amount to very little. It is naturally in the more distant periods that the line dividing myth from history is most difficult to trace. If, on the whole, the chroniclers agree in their account of events, these are not always attributed to the same Inca. It is not uncommon for some events to have a double use, as it were, and to be told in almost the same manner about two separate reigns. The dynastic lists do not always agree, and father, son, and grandson are sometimes mistaken for one another.

Why blame the native narrators for these uncertainties? Perhaps they were not properly understood, not having been interrogated with the care that Sarmiento and his assistants say they gave to the inquiry, which was carried out on the orders of the viceroy Francisco de Toledo. Few historians treat as entirely historical any accounts of reigns before that of Pachacuti (1438–1471), the first ruler whose exploits are not to some extent tinged with myth. Less than a century separates the death of Pachacuti

Queru, lacquered wooden beaker, colonial period

from that of his great-grandson Atahuallpa, strangled by Pizarro in 1533. However imperfect the collective memory may be, it is probable that the exploits of the four successors of Pachacuti belong to a genuine historical tradition, particularly if it is true that a body of men was dedicated to the task of seeing that the memory of it was not lost.

In 1840 and 1888 the manuscript of a Spanish monk, Montesinos, was published, and introduced a certain amount of confusion into the historiography of ancient Peru. This account was written between 1636 and 1642, a century after the conquest, and gives a list of no less than ninety-three emperors who preceded the Incas over a period of four thousand years—Peru being, according to Montesinos, none other than Solomon's kingdom of Ophir. The long chronology of Montesinos' kings, though placed in a distant era, all have Quechua names which are often historical names of the fifteenth century A.D. The silence of the oldest and most reputable chroniclers on this subject and the fabulous nature of these prehistoric annals have given Montesinos a bad reputation. Nevertheless the mystery persists. This pre-Incaic dynasty could not have been entirely made up by Montesinos. He probably used a manuscript left by Father Blas Valera at the Jesuit monastery at La Paz. Now Blas Valera, the son of a conquistador and an Indian woman from Chachapoyas, is no negligible authority. Garcilaso de la Vega frequently quotes him, and other chroniclers lament the loss of his manuscripts. Some modern historians have asked if Montesinos had not somehow miraculously saved from oblivion the names of the rulers of that megalithic empire of which the Incas later became the heirs. However, today the "megalithic" theory has been quite abandoned and few anthropologists believe in the existence of these lost kingdoms, the accounts of which are supposed to have survived in the memories of some bard or "quipu master." The difficulty has been overcome to some extent by postulating that Montesinos had arranged a list of local chiefs or contemporary minor kings in chronological order. It is even possible that the author of the manuscript used by Montesinos may have done the same.

If Montesinos' manuscript is of little value from the historical point of view, it is nonetheless important for what it tells us of the cosmogonic ideas of the Incas. The dynasties of the prehistoric kings are divided into periods of a thousand years and at the end of each one some disaster took place. As with the Aztecs and Mayas, a "Sun" belongs to each of these millennia, and each one has a different human race. The first age was that of the *Wari-Viracocha-runa,* the men of the god Viracocha; the second, that of the *Wari-runa,* the holy men; the third, of the *Purun-runa* or savages; and the fourth, of the *Auka-runa,* the warriors.

These four ages were separated by cataclysms. The end of the first millennium was foreshadowed by strange happenings and followed by catastrophes, such as plagues and wars that depopulated the world. Tools rebelled against their owners, a mythical event which is depicted in a fresco of the Mochica period.

"The Sun got tired of its journeying" at the end of the second epoch "and for twenty hours refused its light to man. The Indians prayed, calling on their father the Sun. They made great sacrifices. . . ." No doubt mankind was consumed by the divine fire.

The third age ended with a flood. No cosmic disaster ended the fourth; men became soft, effeminate, and addicted to sodomy. They were redeemed by the founder of the Inca dynasty, who inaugurated the fifth Sun.

Montesinos, unfortunately, did not realize the purely mythical nature of the Blas Valera records he used. Into a cosmogonical account he has introduced imaginary rulers' names, a kind of doubling of the actual Inca names with various epithets added to them. For good measure he has included some names of animals and places.

Other chroniclers' texts on pre-Incaic times have only a faint echo of this mythology. To exalt the Incas the native informants painted the pre-Incaic picture in the most somber tones. Men lived in caves, were savages, cannibals, and endowed with every vice. War was the natural state of that society, which it was the task of the Incas to civilize. In this imaginary picture of life before the Incas it can be seen that more than a few details were derived from the life of the Amazonian forest tribes, whose country started near Cuzco and who were so much despised by Spaniards and Incas alike. The intertribal wars of the mountain peoples before they were pacified and incorporated into the empire may have helped to suggest the ideas that the Cuzco aristocracy had of those distant times.

Now let us see what can be gleaned from the classical traditions that will throw any light on the origins of the Incas. The *ayllu,* the lines of descent or clans that made up the many agrarian communities of ancient Peru, claimed to have emerged originally from their *pakarina*, a lake, a rock, or a cave, which became their cult object. After four centuries of Christianity the modern Indians still remember these sites. The Incas put their place of origin at Paccari-tambo, eighteen miles southeast of Cuzco. Their ancestors emerged from "three windows," no doubt three caves. From the middle window came four brothers, Ayar Manco, Ayar Cachi, Ayar Uchu, and Ayar Auca, and their sisters, who also were their wives. The Ayar brothers moved toward the Cuzco valley, followed by ten families who had come out of the caverns on either side; from time to time they paused a year or two on their way and at each halt they founded a village. Ayar Manco, better known as Manco Capac, managed to get rid of his brothers by various tricks; one of them was turned to stone and became the idol Huanacuari, presiding, in the imperial era, over the initiation rites of the young nobles. In sole command of the expedition, Manco Capac stopped in the Cuzco valley at the place where a gold rod, which he threw from time to time to test the nature of the soil, embedded itself deep in the earth. He built a hut there with a thatched roof, at a spot where the future Temple of the Sun, the palace of gold, was to rise. The inhabitants of the area by no means welcomed the invaders, but in view of Manco Capac's spirited defense they gave up trying to drive them out.

Here the memory of early migrations is combined with myths explaining the origin of national shrines. The Ayars were gods or demons. One of them, Ayar Cachi, "was so skilled in the use of the sling that with each stone he threw he destroyed a mountain and formed a valley." This is why all valleys in this area were said to have been made by Ayar Cachi and his sling stones. Ayar Auca was a winged genie who was turned into a stone idol, as were his brothers.

Manco Capac belongs to that vast pantheon of mythological persons placed by all Indian peoples at the dawn of their history. They are civilizers as well as being, by turn, gods, heroes, and great ancestors. In another version of this myth, given by Garcilaso de la Vega, Manco Capac is seen as the civilizing hero, Son of the Sun, who came from the borders of Lake Titicaca and took possession of the Cuzco valley in order to teach the rude inhabitants the value of an ordered life. He was turned to stone in the same way as his brothers and became an idol.

Manco Capac's successor was Sinchi Roca. In the first half of this name we find the noun *sinchi*, which once meant warrior chief. This is significant, because the first six or seven Incas were no more than *sinchis* engaged in raiding their neighbors or defending themselves from outside attacks. These obscure skirmishes, this series of feuds, never led to a conquest. It was only in the reign of Yahuar Huacac, in the second half of the fourteenth century, that the Incas, led by two able commanders who were cousins or brothers of the emperor, overcame the inhabitants of the Cuzco valley. Under Viracocha, the next emperor, the country had become sufficiently powerful to intervene in the quarrels between two important kingdoms.

A disaster which might have destroyed the budding power of the Incas forever was the origin of the glorious career of Pachacuti and of the series of conquests which made a small agricultural state into a great empire. The immediate northern neighbors of the Incas were the Quechuas, to whom they were linked by language and also, no doubt, by a similar way of life. Beyond them, while the Inca state was growing, lay the confederation of Chanca tribes, who were developing along the same lines. Their territory was roughly the land between the Pampa and Mantaro rivers, or the provinces of Huancavelica, Ayacucho, and Apurímac. Today, the descendants of the Chancas cannot be distinguished from other Andean Indians. We do not know to what linguistic group they belonged; however, it seems that the Soras, one of their tribes, used to speak an Aymara dialect.

We know very little about the Chanca kingdom, once so greatly feared, but it was made up of two sections, one might say halves, each being ruled by a different chief, protected in battle by the image of his divine ancestor.

At the beginning of the fifteenth century, the Chanca confederation grew proud of its military might and started a series of wars of conquest. Even setting aside the tradition that these Chanca Indians challenged the Chiriguanos in the south of Bolivia, it is nevertheless true that they were imbued with so fierce an urge to expand that they would have founded a veritable empire had they not been broken by Yupanqui Pachacuti.

The Chancas caused the Incas anxiety from the moment they

destroyed their allies and rampart on the eastern border—the Quechuas. The Incas were well aware of the threat of such neighbors and sought allies. In the last years of the Inca Viracocha's reign the Chancas invaded their neighbors' territory. The Inca, enfeebled by age, thought resistance was not possible and, accompanied by his son Urco, took refuge in a fortress above the village of Calca. Contrary to custom he had decided to make Urco his heir.

At this moment another of his sons, the Inca Yupanqui, the future Pachacuti, undertook the defense of Cuzco, helped by two generals, Vicaquirao and Apo-mayta, and a handful of nobles. Unaided by his father and almost without an army, Yupanqui was only feebly supported by the valley peoples whom he had asked for troops. The Chancas, who had advanced as far as Cuzco without opposition, were nevertheless defeated there and their chief killed. Legend attributes this unexpected victory to a miraculous army the Creator raised from the soil by turning stones into men. These supernatural reinforcements, on turning back again to simple stones, became a very special kind of god, the *pururauka*. The Inca Viracocha was far from pleased at this son's triumph; he was in fact filled with anger and tried to kill him, fearing that his glory would prevent, the accession of his favorite son, the Inca Urco. Yupanqui, in spite of the scruples with which the chroniclers credit him, proclaimed himself Inca while his father was still living, and took the name Pachacuti, the "transformer." His only dangerous rivals were the Collas in the Titicaca basin. Their descendants, the Aymara Indians, are particularly known for their military spirit and courage. Before the agricultural reforms of 1953, which put an end to the hacienda system, their revolts were frequent; though armed only with slings, they had no hesitation in facing the government troops. To a great extent it was they who brought about the victory of the Revolutionary Party of Victor Paz Estenssoro, onetime President of Bolivia, and they helped him crush several *pronunciamientos* which would have meant a return to the past. At the time of Pachacuti, the Aymaras or Collas, no doubt descendants of the builders of Tiahuanaco, were divided into little chiefdoms, each trying to dominate the whole area: an endemic state of war prevailed which Pachacuti alone

Map of Cuzco

succeeded in stopping. After his victory over the most powerful of the Aymara *sinchis*, the conquest of the rest of the region was no more than a military walkover. From Collao the Inca marched on Arequipa and brought all the native tribes under subjection as far as the coast.

An army commanded by Capac Yupanqui, the Inca's brother, was sent north. It contained a big contingent of Chanca troops who fought courageously and loyally for the Incas under the command of one of their chiefs. Their military success alarmed even the Inca, who ordered their extermination, but the Chancas got news of this and fled to east Jauja, as far as Cajamarca. According to tradition Pachacuti ordered the execution of the general responsible for this victory, on his return, for having exceeded the limits given him for his campaign. True or not, the incident does show what importance the Incas attached to discipline.

But it is not so much his conquests as the laws and administrative measures of all sorts he introduced that made Pachacuti the greatest of the Incas. Tradition credits him with building so

49

Machu Picchu

many palaces, fortresses, and temples, and with passing so many wise laws that Pachacuti the historical personage has become obliterated by the picture of Pachacuti the mythical hero. After his victory he reconstructed Cuzco on a magnificent scale. The Temple of the Sun, symbolizing the power and wealth of the Incas in the same way as Solomon's temple did that of the Jews, was rebuilt by him.

After a reign of more than thirty years, during which Pachacuti had conducted many wars, built a capital and formed a state, he handed over power to his son, Topa Inca Yupanqui, about the year 1471. The austere Sarmiento, the inveterate collector of historical traditions, has translated a short poem which Pachacuti is said to have recited "in a low, sad voice just before his end":

> Like a lily in the garden was I born
> And like a lily I grew up.
> As the years passed I grew old,
> And when the time for dying came,
> I withered and I died.

Topa Yupanqui was worthy of his father. He extended the empire in the north and added to it most of the territory that is today the Republic of Ecuador. During this campaign he subjugated the redoubtable Cañaris, who later furnished him with a *corps d'élite*, comparable to the Swiss Guard. After the conquest, the Cañaris gave their allegiance to the Spaniards and helped them conquer their former masters, the Incas.

Topa Yupanqui overcame the Chimu kingdom without much difficulty and at the same time took the whole coast as far south as Lima. There is a tradition of a maritime excursion under this Inca to islands inhabited by black men. This has been enough to give rise to the idea that he was the discoverer of Melanesia, but no one who knows the Pacific could imagine an Indian army crossing the ocean on rafts and coming back, against wind and current, to its port of departure. The Spaniards, like modern historians, identified these mysterious islands conquered by Topa Yupanqui as the Galapagos archipelago, although it was uninhabited when discovered in 1535. The potsherds collected there by Thor Heyerdahl show, if not an occupation, at least sporadic visits from coastal Indians, but the small size of these fragments and the lack of any particular character in their ornamentation lend no support to this hypothesis.

The most far-flung and the boldest campaign launched by Topa Yupanqui took him to Chile where, in spite of the resistance of the fierce Araucan Indians, he penetrated as far as the river Maule, which he made the southern frontier of the empire. It was the Inca's last campaign, for he died in 1493, a year after the discovery of America. Apart from his conquests, one of the greatest of Topa Yupanqui's claims to fame is the building of the fortress of Sacsahuamán.

Topa Yupanqui's successor was Huayna Capac, "the young chief rich in virtues." If his career was less brilliant than that of his father it was not so much that his conquests did not equal those of his predecessor, or for any want of skill or ambition, but a lack of worlds to conquer. The Araucan forests, thousands of miles from Cuzco, and similar forests on the eastern slopes of the Andes were two barriers the highlanders hardly dreamed of crossing.

Huayna Capac also had to put down some rebellions. In the Quito region one of them led him into a war against several war-like tribes on the borders of Ecuador and Colombia. After several bloody battles Huayna Capac established the empire's northern frontier on the Ancasamaya river, a tributary of the Guaitará in Colombia. He then undertook a campaign against the coastal peoples in Ecuador, whence he returned with a booty of turquoises.

Huayna Capac died in 1527 or 1528, about the time of Pizarro's first landing at Tumbez. One of the Inca's emissaries may even have dined on board Pizarro's ship. The last days of Huayna Capac may well have been saddened by the news he received of these mysterious strangers. If tradition can be believed, he foresaw the approaching end of his dynasty and kingdom.

By the time of Pizarro's third voyage (1531), Peru was in the throes of civil war. Huayna Capac's favorite son, Atahuallpa, with the help of his father's generals, had taken possession of the north of the kingdom and had succeeded in defeating the armies of his half brother, Huáscar; Huáscar had been officially crowned as Inca in Cuzco. While Pizarro was skirmishing against the Indians of the isle of Puná in the Gulf of Guayaquil, and then against the people of Tumbez, Atahuallpa overcame his rival, Huáscar. Atahuallpa, at the head of his army, advanced toward the capital, already in the hands of Quizquiz, one of his generals. A decisive battle had been fought there in which the Inca Huáscar had been captured. This victory assured Atahuallpa of the crown, or *borla*; he was camped with part of his army in the plains of Cajamarca. Pizarro was aware of all this. If at first he had some intention of supporting Huáscar against Atahuallpa, he gave up the idea as soon as he learned that Atahuallpa had won. For him the Inca was now the *señor natural*, the legitimate ruler, with whom he would play out the match he had in mind. He boldly decided to go and meet Atahuallpa who, in the grip of uncertainty, alternately sent Pizarro threats and tokens of friendship. The Spaniards marched south along the great coastal road, whose construction they much admired. They then entered the mountains, scaling them by steep and narrow paths where it would have been easy to stop them. To their great surprise no obstacle was put in their way, and on November 15, 1532, they reached Cajamarca. That very evening Pizarro's brother, Hernando, was sent as an ambassador to Atahuallpa, who promised to visit the Spaniards already installed in the public buildings around Cajamarca's great square.

No other incident in the conquest of the New World can equal in dramatic power the sudden and brutal fall of the Inca empire. The account of it read by the French in the document mentioned above is so factual and exact that the sheet is worth quoting for the benefit of modern man (it could not be otherwise since it is taken from a letter of Francisco Pizarro, now lost). It describes the events of November 16.

The same day Atabalica* directed his course toward the city of Caxalmaca and arrived there in the evening; he being in his litter all decorated with fine gold came to the Governor and brought him several caciques. Several Indians went before him to clean the road, although it was already clean and there was nothing to clear away. After him were others, some of whom sang while others danced: all around him were many Indians called Gandules who were there to guard him, some carrying battle axes and others halberds made of silver and big clubs hanging from their belts. The Governor, seeing that Atabalica was coming to the city, prepared all his men, both on foot and mounted, and divided them into two parties: after that he sent a gentle father of the Dominican order who was called Vincent to the said Atabalica: which father spoke to him carrying in his hand a book, containing the

* Atabalica: an alternative name for Atahuallpa.

53

words of the Evangelists, and he told Atabalica that the things that were written in this book were what God ordered them to do. Then Atabalica said he should show him the book: which he did and as soon as he had it in his hand he threw it on the ground. The said gentle father picked it off the ground and returned to the Governor crying aloud that the faith of Jesus Christ must be heard. At this point the Governor came out fully armed and on foot with a sword and a shield in his hands and with him all the people he had, both on foot and mounted. Reaching the said Atabalica he laid his hand on him and threw him down from where he was and the other Christians there started to put to death all those who carried him and went with bravery into the midst of the army of Indians a large number of whom they put to death, and the battle lasted from vespers until it was night and they took prisoner many of the principal Indians. The despoiling of those that were taken was estimated at 40,000 gold castilles and 30,000 silver marks and even more as night advanced. The said Atabalica seeing himself prisoner and fearing to be put to death promised the Christians to give them a room, filled with gold, twenty feet high and eighteen feet in width, which thing was done as promised, and all the gold that was in that room with other gold that he added to it amounts to 3,000,000 castilles and thereunto he gave more silver than can be counted, of which sum belongs to Your Majesty as your right 300,000 good gold pesos each of these pesos worth 400,000 pesos and 50 maravedis [sic] of which sum Hernando Pizarro is bringing you at this moment 150,000 gold pesos and 5,000 silver marks: he does not bring more because there are no ships in which he could carry it. It is so marvelous to hear that in dividing this treasure each horseman had as his share 10,000 gold castilles and 350 silver marks and each foot soldier 5,000 gold castilles and 265 silver marks.

Atahuallpa's behavior remains an enigma to this day. Why did he allow a handful of Spaniards to cross his country, making all sorts of depredations, and by what aberration did he allow himself to fall into the obvious trap that was laid for him? Perhaps it can be explained if we look at it from the Indian point of view.

First of all, we must reject the theory that Atahuallpa regarded the strange newcomers as gods, or even supermen. The horses, the arquebuses, and the writing certainly made a great impression on him, but he had discovered that the Spaniards were vulnerable. His spies assured him that, unsaddled, the horses were no longer dangerous and that the arquebuses took a long time to reload. These bearded men, whose appearance more than anything else excited his curiosity, were mortals who could be resisted. What preoccupied Atahuallpa and upset his calculations was the part they had taken in the civil war he had waged against his brother. The Spaniards, in deposing his governors, had favored his rival, but at the same time they had proclaimed their respect for the Inca and their desire to meet him. There is no doubt that it was in the hope of getting them on his side that he allowed this little body of men to approach, secure in the belief that he could easily wipe them out at any moment he chose. His chief mistake was ever to have gone to the square at Cajamarca. If he arrived there only in the evening, though Pizarro was expecting him at noon, it was because he thought the horses, the main advantage the whites had over him, could not be used after sunset. Like most Indians, Atahuallpa does not seem to have doubted that the Spaniards he had met were but an advance guard. He could scarcely conceive of them getting reinforcements from the sea, because up to then the coastal peoples had been reduced to their own meager resources and had all been powerless to oppose the mountain empires.

His second mistake was in hoping to appease the Spaniards by giving them gold. Perhaps he found out too late that it merely increased their appetite for it. Having obtained all he could by holding the person of Atahuallpa, Pizarro had him killed, granting him, in return for his conversion *in extremis* to Christianity, the privilege of being strangled instead of being burned alive. Did Pizarro really believe in an uprising in favor of his prisoner? Did he think him too proud to become a mere puppet king? Did he yield to the demands of Almagro, who wanted to get rid of a hostage that seemed the exclusive property of his comrade and rival? After Pizarro had executed Atahuallpa, accused of "usurpation, fratricide, idolatry, polygamy, and rebellion," he wore mourning and affected great sorrow.

The disintegration of the empire after the death of Atahuallpa emphasizes the rigidity and weakness of the Inca state. Without its head the administrative machine could no longer function, or could function only in a vacuum.

The defeat inflicted on Atahuallpa's army and the massacre that followed filled the Indians with terror. For a long time officers and soldiers were paralyzed. Many, rather than fight against the Spaniards, judged it prudent to serve under their banner. When the Spaniards left Cajamarca to make their grand entry into Cuzco they were accompanied by an army of servants and auxiliaries. They also took with them a brother of Atahuallpa, the young Tupac Huallpa, whom they had made emperor in the hope of conciliating the Indians. Tupac Huallpa died on the journey, poisoned, it is said, by the general Chalicuchima, who hoped to throw off the Spanish yoke. The old warrior was denounced and burned alive. The drama at Cajamarca marks the real end of the Inca empire, in spite of the violent spasms which were still to shake the headless body.

In less than a century the Inca empire, by means of incessant wars, spread out to cover an area of 380,000 square miles, an area about the combined size of the Low Countries, France, Switzerland, and Italy. Other conquerors, it is true, have carved out larger empires in a shorter time; but when you journey at mule-slow pace over the Andean plains along the dried bed of a torrent or across the endless coastal deserts, you cannot cease to marvel at the energy of the three great sovereigns who overcame all these obstacles with their armies, traveling from snow-covered peaks to tropical valleys, almost without transition and enduring hunger and thirst, to subdue populations which they dominated solely by their discipline. How can this thirst for conquest be explained? What were the motives of such imperialism? According to Garcilaso de la Vega and other chroniclers, the Incas, like the Europeans, desired only to extend to other countries the benefits of their own superior civilization and religion. This zeal for civilization and religion reminds one rather too much of the reasons the Spaniards gave for their actions not to appear suspect. Some chroniclers, Garcilaso chief among them, in their wish to exalt the Incas, have generously imputed to them the noblest and highest motives. But there is no doubt that this great territorial expansion was not caused solely by idealism and concern for man's welfare.

First of all, one conquest leads to another. More than once the Incas were obliged to take the offensive against neighboring tribes, disturbed by the success of the Peruvian armies, in order to ensure the possession of a recently annexed territory. Moreover, armies seasoned by a succession of campaigns could not be left idle without the risk of their losing their ardor for battle. If one may believe the chroniclers, several expeditions were undertaken merely to keep the army in training.

The generals were mostly Incas, near relatives of the emperor, and favored an expansionist policy that brought them glory and wealth. War and religion were the only two careers open to the ambitious in this rigid society. More than one *curaca*, who was not of the imperial line, owed his fortune to his courage or his talents as a strategist.

In default of any precise evidence on the subject, the character of Inca civilization allows us to put forward theories as to the nature of this devouring imperialism. First of all on a psychological level, the Incas, chiefs of warlike tribes, were accustomed to defend themselves against attack by their neighbors and to pillage them whenever the opportunity arose. Ambition, vanity, and personal rivalry may have played a part in first forming the aggressive policy of the Incas. War would then become a type of ideal to which they would conform in order to retain their prestige and dignity. When Pachacuti, after the victory over the Chancas, found himself at the head of enormous resources and numbers of men, the temptation to pay off some old scores without much risk must have been great. Each conquest increased the wealth of the state in lands and tribute. For sovereigns who were such persistent builders, the conquest of a province meant new supplies of soldiers and workmen. As the number of officials needed to run the empire increased, the Inca would have to obtain new lands in order to be able to reward his dignitaries and officers, or to obtain raw materials for the maintenance of his civil service. Above all they wanted primary products—gold, silver, feathers of tropical birds—for the use of craftsmen working at court or in the service of the provincial governors. Though, as we shall see, tribute was paid mostly in personal service, yet it also included material considered precious or essential for the Inca economy.

To secure peace in their kingdom, the Incas were at times obliged to make war beyond the frontiers established by their predecessors or by themselves. Revolts were frequently started with the complicity of still independent tribes. Although we can only guess, it may well be that the Incas counted among the advantages of war the opportunity it gave them of carrying off Indians from their villages and turning them into *yanas*, servants or tenants of the Inca or his nobles. However, the Inca civilization never knew slavery as such, though the condition of the *yanacuna* approached it.

Armies were recruited in the same way as gangs of workers. The numbers of troops conscripted in the provinces were based on the size of the adult population. The decimal system, which was used in the administration, was also applied to the division of the army and to the hierarchy. Discipline was severe. Atahuallpa condemned to death all those Indians who had flinched with fear at their first sight of horses the evening of Fernando Pizarro's visit. Looters were severely punished and the Spaniards, who pillaged among the best, were astonished that, in their adversary's army, the theft even of a cob of maize was the subject of a severe reprimand. These large armies were supplied without great difficulty, thanks to the government stores distributed along the roads. These included not only abundant food, but also equipment such as sandals, clothes, and weapons.

The soldiers were grouped according to their arms. Those provincial contingents that were considered the most trustworthy were placed nearest to the Inca during marches and battle. As missile weapons the Inca troops had the sling, the spear thrower, and the *bolas,* three stone balls joined by cords. This last weapon, much used by huntsmen, was particularly effective against the Spanish cavalry. The bow and arrow were not employed by the highlanders, but the auxiliaries from the "hot lands" of Amazonia were equipped with them. For hand-to-hand fighting the soldiers used wooden swords with sharpened edges, clubs with a stone or metal head bristling with spikes, bronze halberds and pikes. The Inca soldiers protected themselves by means of square or round shields, helmets, and cloth tunics stuffed with cotton. This armor was held by the Spaniards to be so effective that they adopted it themselves for use in their battles against the Indians.

As conquerors the Incas seem to have shown exemplary moderation and wisdom. Before starting a war, the Inca always sent an ambassador to the chiefs of the nation or tribe he was preparing to conquer to invite them "in the Name of the Sun to acknowledge his authority, upon which they would be treated with honor and loaded with presents." These promises, to which were added terrible threats against the obstinate, often resulted in the submission of entire provinces without the loss of a drop of

Inca storehouse, Incahuasi

blood. It is not possible to doubt the unanimous evidence of the Spanish chroniclers, for an administrative document with no literary pretensions confirms it. When Spanish civil servants in the Chincha valley were collecting information about the domination of the Incas the natives said that

a hundred and fifty years ago, an Inca arrived and conquered them in the following way: he said he was Son of the Sun, come to them for their good and the good of all. He wanted neither silver, nor gold, nor women, nor anything they possessed, because he had them all in abundance and he even brought goods to give them. He asked them to accept him as lord and gave them clothes, golden jewelry, and many other things they lacked. The *curacas* of the region assembled and welcomed him as lord and protector by reason of the good treatment he had meted out to them.

Though the Incas might prefer diplomacy and gentleness to violence, they were nonetheless ferocious when resisted. The story of their conquests abounds in bloody episodes; whole tribes were slaughtered and any survivors deported.

On the return from a victorious campaign the Inca would celebrate his triumph. The soldiers entering Cuzco brandished the heads of the vanquished on their pikes. Those adversaries who had particularly roused the wrath of the Inca were skinned and the skins made into drums, "which kept the human shape so well that the dead man seemed to be beating his own belly with drumsticks placed in his hands, or to be playing a flute." Skulls were made into cups from which *chicha* was drunk. At Cajamarca a Spaniard found a skull lined with gold and fitted with a little drinking tube, also in gold. Pizarro asked Atahuallpa what this object was for, and he replied, "It is the skull of one of my brothers who fought against me and boasted that he would drink maize beer from my head. I had him killed and it is I who drink from his." He ordered the cup filled with *chicha* and drank it in front of everybody. Necklaces were made from the teeth of enemies. In 1616, the descendants of the Incas, who in that year reconstructed certain episodes of their old wars to the glory of Saint Ignacio de Loyola, exhibited a necklace "made from teeth their ancestors had torn from the captains of conquered nations."

The Peasants of the Andes

The Incas' power rested on the work and union of many peoples, who, though they spoke different languages and had different ways of life, were nevertheless part of an appreciably uniform civilization. The empire was a mosaic made up of nations and tribes, among whom could be found ancient kingdoms such as the Chimu, confederations of tribes, and primitive and isolated groups.

When the Incas described to the Spaniards, who were anxious to know about their past, the many chaotic groups from which their ancestors had succeeded in molding a single state, they harked back, no doubt, to the little rural communities of the Andes valleys, the *ayllus*, which, at that distant time, enjoyed a certain autonomy and in fact constituted the true nucleus of the empire. Families making up an *ayllu* claimed a common ancestor and thus considered themselves to be of the same blood. One of the oldest Inca dictionaries translates the word *ayllu* as "tribe, genealogy, house, family." In spite of this real or fictitious relationship, the members of an agrarian community married for

61

The Indian still uses the Inca digging stick—the *tajilla*

preference among themselves, though there was no formal pro-
hibition against taking an outsider to wife. Thus the *ayllu* was
less a clan, in the strict sense of the term, than a great patrilinear
group owning a parcel of agricultural land, the *marka;* this
brought the community together, which action was reinforced by
mutual obligations, beliefs and common traditions, and the worship of the same protective gods. The ancestor, sometimes thought
of as an animal, was more often identified as some natural object,
often a rock of more or less strange shape standing near a mountain, cave, or lake. One cannot conclude from this that the Peruvians were totemic, for these myths about their origins were not
accompanied by any of those practices which elsewhere character-
ize totemism.

If one may believe the Indians who described the state of Peru
before the Inca conquest to the inquisitors of Francisco de
Toledo, each of these communities was independent and endowed with such a perfectly democratic organization that in time
of peace there was no chief to obey. "There was no other government," one of these informants tells us,

> than the gallant captains called *sinchis,* who commanded and governed
> when they made war on each other, entering one another's territory to
> steal fodder, wood, or other things. The war once over, these captains
> were no more important than the rest of the Indians. They were not
> looked up to and had no power or commandment over the people. . . .

It is probable that in many regions of Peru rural communities
ruled themselves, merely nominating, at the most, temporary
chieftains. The appointment of village authorities no doubt depended then, as now, on a council of heads of families which, in
effect, never met, but made its decisions somewhat by chance as
the result of casual talks and more or less fortuitous meetings.

However, if things were this way and these communities lived
under a system of idyllic equality, how does one explain the existence of hereditary chieftains, the *curacas,* elders, who were incorporated in due course into the Inca political system and who,
after the Spanish conquest, hurried to claim their ancient rights
over the community? Few historians seem to have noticed the
contradiction. There are constantly to be found, in the administrative documents of the age, all sorts of questions about more or

less powerful overlords whom the Incas had either deposed or confirmed in their positions. Society, consequently, cannot have been as democratic as one might suppose from the evidence of other sources. In reality, social and political conditions varied from one valley to the next. In one the *ayllu* would recognize only the authority of the "elders" or a village headman; in another they obeyed a chief who had succeeded in establishing his rule over several *ayllus,* thus becoming a petty king. The *curacas* owned land which the village community was obliged to till and they could, at will, raise men for war or for works to benefit the community.

The true owner of the soil was the clan, which owned cultivable land and jealously preserved its boundaries against encroachment. Inside this social and geographical framework, each family had its rights, the precise nature of which we do not know. Sometimes the lands were passed down by inheritance into the same family, at other times plots were periodically redistributed according to the needs of each family group. Such lots would be bigger or smaller according to the number and sex of individuals in each household. The evidence for an annual redistribution of land is given by too many authorities for it to be denied, but landed property is attested to no less categorically. Perhaps certain modern customs will help us to reconcile these contradictions. In some Peruvian *comunidades,* particularly for instance at Kauri, there is an annual symbolic redistribution of the lands which, in fact, in no way changes the existing situation. The heads of families affirm their rights by going around their fields and treading the soil in front of the authorities. In other places, agrarian communities dispose of fallow or uncultivated land by bestowing it on young households or on those who undertake to pay for a religious feast. At one time members of a community unable to work their fields for a time did not forfeit their rights; their lands were cultivated by the community as were those of widows and the infirm. Everyone could lead his flock to graze on the common pasture, and draw on the other resources of the territory. These groups were self-sufficient in all essentials and only exchanged a few natural products, or manufactured articles, with their neighbors. Craft specialization, such as it was, was due either to some local cultural tradition, or to

64

Yesterday's village and today's

the easy accessibility of certain raw materials.

The *ayllus,* or agrarian communities, were grouped in "halves," called *hanan-saya,* upper half, and *hurin-saya,* lower half. This bipartite division is especially familiar to us because Cuzco was made up of two sections, Hanan Cuzco and Hurin Cuzco. The first Inca sovereigns belonged to the families of the lower half "until the advent of Inca Roca who, as a result of a palace revolution, transferred to the upper half the privilege of counting the Inca and his family among its members." Although the religious or social functions of the "halves" are not very clear, nevertheless this dualist organization, found in many primitive populations of the Americas, exists to this day. During fiestas at

65

Cuzco, the members of the two halves assemble separately, and a certain rivalry or emulation between them can still be seen when the *hanan-saya* and the *hurin-saya* celebrate their patron saint's feast day. The ritual feasts sometimes degenerate into brutal fights.

These little rural communities, which we have tried to reconstruct, prospered and multiplied thanks to an intensive agriculture and to stock raising. In no other part of the world has man culled so many different kinds of plant, wild or cultivated, as in Peru. It has been estimated that the natives grew more than forty varieties in their fields for food, medical, or manufacturing purposes. Such an abundance is only to be explained by the great range of climates within a restricted area, by the number of different cultures that came together in the melting pot before they fused into this vast community, and lastly, by the constant attention paid to agriculture for thousands of years.

The potato is the most precious gift Peru has given to the Old World. By patience and long trial and error the Indians changed the wild tubers, bitter, hard-skinned, and scarcely bigger than a nut, into one of our favorite foods. It is difficult to imagine how the high plateau could have been peopled, or great civilizations such as the Tiahuanaco could have arisen, without the potato. The Indians had been able to select out of a large number of varieties (about 700), adapted to different uses and climatic zones, those suitable for the high altitudes. Though the potato played a big part in native diet, its importance was always inferior to that of maize, which, though it had come late on the scene, was the noble food and the only one worthy of being offered to the gods.

The cereal used on the high plateaus was quinoa, the mountain rice, rich in proteins and minerals, a plant that stands up to frost and hail. As one comes down to the hot lands the number of cultivated plants grows all the time: squashes, pimiento, haricot beans, ʃweet potatoes, manioc, groundnuts, tomatoes, avocado pears, and cotton are but the most important. The extraordinary development of Andean agriculture is all the more remarkable in so rugged a country where flat surfaces, suitable for cultivation, are comparatively rare. By tremendous effort the Indians

66

Cultivation terraces

succeeded in increasing the arable area by terracing the mountainsides, even the steepest, where it looks as if gigantic staircases run from the bottom of a valley to the snowline.

Cultivation of the highlands depends to a great extent on irrigation because of both the long dry season and the rapid evaporation of rain water. The Incas undertook tremendous irrigation works. In an excess of enthusiasm Garcilaso de la Vega says "they are superior to the most marvelous work there is in the world." Like him we find it hard to understand "how with no iron or steel tools, using huge stones and their unaided arms alone, the Indians were able to construct such works; how they were able to overturn immense rocks, ascend rivers to their source to avoid the deeps, and cross the highest mountains."

Today the traces of their canals can be followed for dozens of

Irrigation channel cut in rock, Cajamarca

miles and some of them cover much greater distances, even if the hundreds of leagues of Garcilaso are an exaggeration. These channels crossed gorges on masonry aqueducts and penetrated mountain spurs by tunnels. At Cajamarca a canal was cut in the living rock for more than half a mile and the engineers gave it a zigzag course to slow down the flow of the water. At Huandoval, two canals meet between two mountains and cross each other. One of them, four and a half feet wide, runs along the top of a wall while the other flows at a right angle to it. According to Wiener, to whom we owe the description of this work, there used to be a third canal, now dry, beneath the other two levels.

The Indians had no hesitation in damming rivers or in correcting or even turning their courses. The water, stored in reservoirs or cisterns, was distributed by sluices. The Incas' scientific knowledge, though quite empirical, was considerable, judging by the art with which they gauged the angle of a gradient and made use of rivers and lakes, often collecting the waters at the foot of glaciers.

The coastal people had long used the immense deposits of

guano for their agriculture—the product which, in the last century, has made Peru rich. It is even possible that this wonderful fertilizer was carried into the interior of old Peru, because, according to Garcilaso de la Vega, the Inca "gave the guano islands to any province he pleased and the distribution of the guano was made with such care that not only no town, but no single inhabitant, could complain." The seabirds whose droppings form the guano were protected by strict laws; it was forbidden "under pain of death to visit the island during the egg-laying season, or to kill the birds anywhere wheresoever."

The domestication of the llama and the alpaca gave the Peruvian economy a unique character among the nations of the New World. On the high plateaus, where the yield of crops is precarious and low due to storms and altitude, the Indians led an entirely pastoral life. Moreover, these people were by no means the poorest. They obtained all they needed by trading the wool and meat of their flocks. The llama was the beast of burden. Although it refuses to carry a load of more than fifty-five pounds and does not travel more than about ten miles per day, its extreme frugality compensates for these drawbacks. The economic value of the alpaca resides chiefly in its thick fleece.

Houses, standing alone or grouped into hamlets or villages, generally occupied rocky or infertile land in order to preserve the good land for agriculture. They were usually placed halfway up a mountain slope, between the hot or temperate lands in the bottom of the valley and the pastures around the summit. By this midway situation the Indians were enabled to grow crops suited to a number of climates, to vary their food, and to avoid a total loss of crops in the event of some disaster.

Many households, closely related to each other and under the authority of an "elder," lived in neighboring huts set around a sort of courtyard. The shape and structure of these buildings varied according to region. In the central Andean valleys they were rectangular and made of cob, turves, or dry stone walling and covered with thatch. Inside, a few niches served as cupboards, for they had almost no furniture. The Indians slept on the ground, wrapped in a big woolen blanket. Guinea pigs ran freely about the room or were put into a shallow trench. An enclosure outside held the few llamas to which the family was entitled.

In a people as deeply attached to their fields as were the Andean Indians, religion naturally took on a strongly agricultural character. Though little is known about the calendar of village fetes, it cannot have differed much from that of the Incas, which closely followed the rhythm of the seasons and the work in the fields. Despite its great pomp, the imperial religion was dominated by the same concerns and desires as was that of the remotest village. It is not chance that the principal pagan god still venerated by the Incas' descendants is Pacha-mama, the Earth Mother, who gives or withholds her blessings to her children and watches over their flocks. The beliefs, religious rites, and peasant magic that the Spanish missionaries tried in vain to eliminate are attributed to the Inca civilization only because our knowledge of them goes no further back. In fact, they were no doubt common to the majority of Andean tribes well before their unification under a single dynasty. It will be best to discuss these beliefs here in order to complete our picture of rural life.

As the Spanish priests particularly sought out the idols, those tangible evidences of paganism, we are better informed about their worship than about any other aspect of the Indian religion. To help the ecclesiastical "visitor" to do away with idolatry, priests retiring from this work would write little guides for the use and benefit of their new colleagues. These treatises, together with sermons denouncing popular "superstitions," are full of priceless details on the beliefs and practices dear to the villagers. The Indians gave the general name *huaca* to the idols and the sanctuaries that sheltered them; the word could also mean any object or happening in which they saw something of the supernatural. A *huaca* could as well be a mountain as a plant or some strange animal. An abnormal child, for instance one born with six fingers on a hand, could become a *huaca* in the same way as could a charm. Rock crystals and the famous bezoar stones, the chalky deposits found in the intestines of herbivores, everything in fact, near or far, that suggested the presence of some strange force was a *huaca*. Rural religion, and to some extent that of the Incas themselves, was not far removed from a somewhat crude animism, or even a certain animatism, because it did not always personify the occult force with which certain objects were apparently charged.

The word *huaca,* meaning the sanctuary where the fetishes were worshipped, has also been extended to the old tombs and the funerary urns contained in them. Today the tomb robbers trading in antiquities are called *huaqueros.* It is difficult to establish any hierarchy among the *huacas,* so bitterly denounced by the "visitors," in view of the vagueness of our sources. The worship of the ancestor of the community was very important, as it guaranteed the unity of the group. It symbolized the threads holding families together, without which they would have lost the memory of their common origin. It was their *kamak,* their creator, who had made the laws governing their group. They were credited with having special clothes and customs which distinguished them from others.

In order to reconcile the myth of the creation of all mankind by a single god and the belief in the separate origins of nations or *ayllus,* the Indians imagined that once the Creator, Viracocha, had finished his task, he sent the ancestors of all the peoples below ground. In due course they came out again from a cave, a mountain, a lake, or a tree. "The Indians made these places *huacas,* or sanctuaries, in memory of the first man of their line who had thus emerged." The *pakarina* was not only the mythical ancestor, he was also the place of his appearance and the spot where he was turned to stone. His descendants used to go there to make sacrifices, and regain their powers by contact with beneficent emanations arising from these hallowed places or objects.

The rock which symbolized the community's ancestor, human or animal, was given the name of *markayok,* translated by the Spanish as "patron" or "guardian" of the village. If the object was a movable stone it belonged to the chief of the *ayllu,* who took care of it and left it to his heirs.

Arriaga, the most celebrated of the exterminators of idolatry, says:

After the stone *huacas* their greatest objects of veneration and adoration are the *malquis,* the bones or whole bodies of their pagan ancestors, which they say are sons of the *huaca.* They keep them far from the fields, in *machayes,* which are their old tombs. Sometimes they are covered with precious vestments and feathers of various colors, or fine cloth, called *kumbi.*

71

Tombs in the cliff, Cajamarca

The mythical ancestor, symbolized by a rock or stone, was often confused with these human remains; "the visitors had difficulty in finding out whether the venerated ancestor was a stone or a body."

The dead were put into caves, vaulted tombs, or kinds of round or square towers. They received offerings and sacrifices from their relatives, who asked them for help and advice. It was with the greatest repugnance, not to say horror, that the Indians obeyed the Roman Catholic priests, who insisted that the dead be buried in consecrated ground in cemeteries. Despairingly, they would dig up the bodies at night to carry them to the old tombs. When the Jesuit fathers asked them why they did this they answered, "For pity's sake, and in consideration of our dead, so that they may not be wearied by the weight of earth upon them."

Each family had a number of charms, called *conopas* or *chancas* according to the region, which could rank also as *huacas.* They were of many kinds. The commonest were stones of unusual appearance or color, and were credited with bringing prosperity to the household and with keeping misfortune and sickness away. Certain stones, which happened to look something like a domestic animal or a cultivated plant, were collected and promoted to the position of guardians of the flocks and crops. A little subtle retouching was sometimes done to complete a chance resemblance. The talisman then became a work of art. One should perhaps class as *conopas* those little figurines of llamas, with a deep cavity on the back, found all over the ancient empire. By analogy with a custom preserved to this day, it is supposed that these little figures, containing some offering or other, were buried in the pastures with the object of getting the Earth Mother's blessing for the increase of the flock.

There is no doubt that a relationship exists between the numerous stone effigies of maize cobs, which are such a great feature of archaeological collections, and the ownership of Sara-mama, the "Mother of Maize," who, like the spirit of grain in Europe, becomes incarnate in a sheaf after the harvest. In Peru the Maize Spirit was symbolized by a very large or a twin cob, which was carefully preserved in a miniature granary until the next harvest.

The *conopas* that protected a community were buried in a secret place or hidden in a cleft in the rock. At certain fixed dates the Indians would get them out of these hiding places and make them offerings such as powdered shells, red ocher, little bags of gold or silver, coca leaves, and other substances with magical properties. They burned aromatic herbs in their honor, sprinkled the *conopas* with the blood of their victims, and made fervent prayers to them. Some twenty years ago I was with the Uro-Chipayas Indians and took part in their ceremonies in honor of the *samiris,* simple blocks of stone considered the guardians of the village. Under my very eyes they performed rituals in which it was easy to recognize those that the Spanish inquisitors had denounced so violently.

The Indians also treated as *huacas* those piles of stones, or *apachetas,* that are still found on hilltops or along the roads at spots where travelers are tempted to rest. The Indians never fail to add a stone, which sometimes they have carried on their backs all the way up the mountain. As a mark of respect, they used to pull out a few eyebrow hairs and blow them into the air or leave their wad of coca as an offering. They also left "small splinters of wood, straw, an old shoe, or a piece of rag. These

A modern *huaca* (Chipaya)

stones and sundry articles ended up by forming high piles, on which the Spaniards hurried to plant a cross." On being asked about this custom, the Indians replied that "they recovered their breath and got rid of fatigue." Others said that, if they neglected the *apachetas*, which they "worshipped like a *huaca*," the former would not let them pass on their return.

In the villages, the priests were often members of the community who, because of age, could no longer work in the fields, but who could still be useful through their knowledge of ceremony and tradition. They lived from the produce of the fields dedicated to the gods.

Magicians, whose functions merged with those of the priests and medicine men, were found among those who had been struck by lightning and were thus, obviously, the chosen ones of Illapa, the God of Thunder. They foretold the future, looked after the sick, and conducted private ceremonies. They were also consulted for the purpose of discovering a thief or punishing him by means of magic charms.

By the side of these tutelary gods, represented by fetishes, were a crowd of evil spirits and supernatural monsters, still remembered in today's folklore. We find mention even in the sixteenth century of the *hapiñuñu*, a woman with long falling breasts, with which she caught solitary travelers to devour them; there were flying heads which planted their teeth in their victims' necks and sucked the blood, also the *anchanchu*, which fed on the fat of people it surprised by night.

The souls of the dead left their old familiar places with regret. Jealous, or afraid of solitude, they tried to take the soul of some relative with them; for this reason a bed of ash was laid around a house, so that the footprints of those whom the dead wanted to draw to them could be seen.

The Inca Caste

The keystone of the empire was the *Sapa Inca,* that is, the emperor, directly descended from Inti, the Sun God, and sharing his divinity. To this day, among the poorest and most ignorant Indians the word Inca evokes a vague image of a mysterious and benevolent being. The Spaniards vied with one another in extolling the splendor of his court, the respect with which he was surrounded, and the pride of his spirit. But more moving to us are the remarks of the few Spaniards who accompanied Hernando de Soto and Hernando Pizarro when they went as ambassadors to Atahuallpa, camped on the Cajamarca plain. They were both the first and the last men of our race to have seen the Inca at the height of power, undisputed sovereign of an immense country. The next day this monarch was no more than a humiliated prisoner, destined to be strangled.

The emperor had set up his headquarters near a sulphur spring, beside which were some buildings where he resided. There was a swimming pool there, fed by two conduits, one of hot water and the other of cold. He liked to bathe there in the

Head, Inca period

company of the women of his harem. When the Spaniards arrived in his presence, Atahuallpa, his forehead bound with the *maskapaicha*, a red fringe, was seated on a small canopied stool made of wood, surrounded by his women and a great number of dignitaries, each in his allotted place according to rank. Two women had stretched in front of the Inca a piece of cloth, through which he could see without being seen himself, "according to the custom of these lords, who rarely allowed their vassals to look on them." Hernando de Soto having insisted that this cloth be lowered, Atahuallpa, his head bent, affected not to look at him and communicated with his questioner by means of a herald. He talked directly to Hernando Pizarro only when he was told that the Spaniard was the brother of the *apo*, the strangers' chief.

The Inca was so careful of his dignity that he remained unmoved when Hernando de Soto reared his horse so close to him that the froth from the animal's mouth fell on the emperor's clothes. All the guards who had flinched on seeing this unknown monster bearing down on them were executed that night, together with all their families. At the end of the interview, Atahuallpa had *chicha* served in two gold cups, one of which he offered to Hernando Pizarro while he emptied the other. He did the same with de Soto, but with silver cups. The Indians today drink the health of their guests in the same way.

Early in the afternoon of the next day, Atahuallpa set off in great state toward the town of Cajamarca.

First of all appeared a squadron of Indians in checkered uniforms of different colors. They moved forward taking up any bits of straw that lay on the road, and sweeping it clean. Next came three squadrons variously clothed, dancing and singing, then a number of men wearing armor made of large plates of gold and crowned with gold and silver. In their midst was Atahuallpa, carried in a litter decorated with parrot feathers of various colors and gold and silver plates; it was carried by numerous Indians. He was followed by two litters each bearing an important cacique and finally there were several companies of Indians with gold and silver crowns. (Pedro Pizarro)

The richness of the bodyguard made a tremendous impression on the Spaniards, and another witness of this event, Estete, confirms this, saying, "They were covered with so many plates of

Detail from a *queru,* dance with the golden chain

gold and silver that it was marvelous to see them glittering in
the sun."

This magnificent sight was not specially staged to impress the
Spaniards with the might and grandeur of the Inca. We know
from other sources that the Inca never moved about except in
great state, in a litter the poles of which were encrusted with
gold and silver and "surmounted with two jeweled arches, holding up heavy curtains which hid the sovereign from the sight of
the people." Archers and halberdiers surrounded the royal litter,
and they were preceded and followed by a veritable army.
Couriers announced the approach of the emperor, and the crowds
massed along the route cried out as he passed, "Oh, great and
very powerful Lord, Son of the Sun, only ruler, may all the
earth obey you." Cieza de León, to whom we owe these details,
says, "He fell little short of being adored as a god."

The sacred character of the Inca's person showed itself in the
nature of the homage paid to him. The Indians started by
raising their faces and hands to the sun, then doing the same
toward the Inca, saying, "Son of the Sun, friend of the poor."
They left offerings at his feet, even sacrificing llamas to him as
Son of the Sun. (Betanzos)

Over the ten months that Atahuallpa remained a prisoner, the
conquistadores often had occasion to remark on the etiquette
used by the women and courtiers who yet remained faithful to
him. Though he had been deceived and humiliated, Atahuallpa
lost none of their respect, a respect close to fear. The Cacique of
Huaylas, who had asked for leave of absence and had returned

80

Inca vessel

later than the date fixed by the emperor, was so overcome at the thought of facing him "that he trembled till he was almost unable to stand." However, when Atahuallpa saw him he (the Inca) "lifted his head, smiled at him, and made a sign to him to leave."

Each of the women of the emperor's harem served him in turn for a week or ten days. Each was accompanied by her attendants, "daughters of lords." Only these women had constant access to the sovereign. The nobles and caciques remained in the courtyard, waiting to be summoned by the emperor. They never went before him except barefoot and carrying a burden on their backs. Even Chalicuchima, the most glorious of Atahuallpa's generals, observed this rule when he "threw himself in tears at the foot of his master."

Atahuallpa ate seated on his stool. His food was served in gold, silver, or pottery vessels, placed before him on little mats. "He indicated the dish that he desired, and one of the women held it in her hands while he ate it." If any of the food fell onto his clothing and stained it, he went to his rooms and changed.

Everything the Inca touched became taboo. Pedro Pizarro saw chests "containing all that Atahuallpa had touched with his hands, and the clothes he had cast off. There were the mats on which he put his feet when eating, the animal or bird's bones he

81

had had in his hands and gnawed, the maize cobs he had thrown aside, in short everything he had touched." Having asked why all this was kept, Pizarro was told "it was in order that they should be burned, for every year everything these Lords, Sons of the Sun, touched had to be burned, and the ashes had to be thrown to the winds, for nobody must touch them." There was a nobleman with these Indians who kept control of all these things collected by the women.

The Inca's clothing differed from that of his subjects only by being made of more finely woven vicuña wool. This same Pedro Pizarro tells how he was struck by the silky quality of a brown cape worn by Atahuallpa, who told him it was woven from bat hair. On seeing his questioner's astonishment he said that the people—dogs he called them—in Tumbez and Puerto Viejo had nothing better to do than catch these creatures to make garments for him.

The symbol of imperial dignity was the *llautu,* plaited cords of different colors going five or six times around the head and leaving a woolen fringe hanging down over the forehead, the *maskapaicha,* each strand of which passed through a small gold tube. There was an upright piece on top crowned with a sort of pompom and three rare bird's feathers. In his ears were enormous golden disks. He also wore a golden disk on his chest and big bracelets. In his hand he carried a star-shaped scepter or a short halberd of gold.

Another symbol of royalty was a white llama, called *napa,* representing the first of these animals to appear on earth after the flood. Its ears were ornamented with jewels in gold settings and its back covered with a scarlet cloth. In April fifteen llamas were sacrificed to it and to the *suntur paukar,* a spear shaft decorated with feathers, which was one of the royal insignia. *Chicha,* from which libations were made, was put into jars which the *napa* then overturned as it moved about. This ceremony shows beyond doubt the sacred nature of these symbols of sovereignty.

The Inca had around him, in addition to his innumerable wives and concubines (more than seven hundred, it is said), a great number of uncles, brothers, cousins, and sons, as well as the sons of petty kings and provincial caciques. He was attended by an army of servants. Among the natives questioned by the viceroy

82

Inca throne, Cuzco

Francisco de Toledo's agents in 1572, to obtain information on the reigns of the Incas, were the sons and grandsons of numerous officers of the court. Among them were chamberlains, keepers of the royal wardrobe, who saw to it that the Inca's clothes fitted him properly, keepers of the vicuña cloth (*kumbi*), suppliers of salt (*cachi-kamayoc*), keepers of the royal insignia (the maces and headbands), gardeners (*chacra-kamayoc*), shepherds, keepers of the royal granaries, and architects. To this list must be added sweepers, water carriers, cooks, and the waiters mentioned by Garcilaso de la Vega. Many of these posts were hereditary. One of the witnesses at the viceroy Toledo's inquiry said, "My father was chamberlain and keeper of the wardrobe for Huayna Capac as his ancestors were for Topa Inca Yupanqui."

The royal litter bearers, who had to have a quick and regular pace, were recruited from the Lucana tribe.

The court domestics had the reputation of being "able and reliable men, good at their work." They were supplied by villages or towns who thereafter became responsible for their conduct. Any serious misdemeanor committed by a servant was expiated by the inhabitants of his place of origin. However humble these posts might be, they were much desired, "because those who held them had the honor of approaching the emperor, and they were entrusted with not only the Inca's home but also his person, which they regarded as the greatest privilege they could obtain."

Toward the end of the dynasty, the principle of the purity of the divine blood that the Incas had inherited from their ancestor, the Sun, was carried to its logical conclusion: the Inca was not allowed to take as his principal wife, his *coya*, any other than his full sister. This extreme form of endogamy was only introduced gradually, for at the start of the dynasty there were Incas who took wives from outside lineages. However, according to the official mythology, Mama Ocllo, the first empress, was also a daughter of the Sun and hence Manco Capac's sister.

The ideas of primogeniture and legitimacy seen from a Spanish point of view have colored, if not falsified, the information we have on the rights of succession among the Incas. The heir presumptive was not necessarily the son of the empress. It even seems that, in the earliest times of the dynasty, the sovereign would indicate the son he thought most suitable to wear the *maskapaicha,* or imperial fringe, among the sons of his numerous wives. In principle all the royal sons had equal rights to the throne, hence the succession led to all kinds of intrigues, rivalries, and revolts and disturbed the beginning of each reign. In the hope of preventing these struggles, the later sovereigns restricted their choice of a successor to the sons of the chief wife, the *coya* or *piui huarmi,* who, at least in principle, was a full sister of the Inca. As an extra precaution, the Inca would associate his chosen heir with the royal power and, while he himself was still alive, would allow his successor to encircle his brow with the scarlet band, the symbol of kingship.

The emperor's heir was, in principle, the one among his sons he judged to be best capable of governing the people. Pachacuti found that his eldest son, Tupac Amaru, whom he wished to make his heir, lacked the qualities of a leader, and obliged him to renounce the throne in favor of his younger son Topa Inca Yupanqui, who had shown himself to be a better general. Other emperors, less conscientious about the public good, allowed themselves to be influenced by the wishes of a favorite woman. The Inca Viracocha, who had shown such cowardice when the Chancas invaded the country, did everything he could to get his son Urco made his successor "because he much loved his mother." The court nobles took the part of Pachacuti, the man who had saved the capital by crushing the Chancas. When this prince made the captives prostrate themselves before his father, so that the old emperor could put his foot ón their necks as a token of their submission, the Inca, in blind obstinacy, insisted that this honor should fall to Urco, who had had no part in the campaign. Viracocha even tried to assassinate Pachacuti, who ended the matter by getting rid of Urco. The Inca Huayna Capac also had to fight against a half brother, to whom his father wanted to leave the throne, even though he was not the son of the *coya.* It was an uncle of Huayna Capac (a full brother) who had him proclaimed emperor, with the help of the Inca nobility. We have already spoken of the disastrous war of succession between Huáscar and Atahuallpa at the time of the Spaniards' arrival. The hatred generated by this rivalry between half brothers was so great that some of the Inca nobles who had supported Huáscar preferred to ally themselves with the Spaniards rather than join with the opposing faction to fight them.

The education of the young nobles and the sons of the *curacas* was put into the hands of the *amautas,* "able men, or those who passed as such." "The duties of these *amautas* were to teach the young nobles the ceremonies and precepts of their religion, the reasons and basis of the law, to instruct them in political and military affairs, to polish their manners, to teach them the history and chronology of the race by means of the knotted cords, to get them to talk well, and to omit nothing necessary to the education of their children and the conduct of the family." It is significant that only Blas Valera and Morua, both late writers, speak of the palace schools. Were they not interpreting in European terms an education based on the example of the older generation and the transmission of oral traditions and rites to those who were destined to play a part in religion or administration?

The heir presumptive learned his duties by watching his father, and gradually assuming a greater share in his military and religious activities. If he was associated with the empire, he would find himself given important tasks, such as undertaking a military campaign or running a province.

With the object of preventing the troubles likely to occur when an emperor died, the Inca was hidden in a building away from the palace, where only those close to him were allowed to come, as soon as his health caused any anxiety. Only good news of his progress was put out by the officers of the court during the whole of his illness. If he died, the news was kept secret for about a month and was only proclaimed when all the provincial governors had been warned and measures taken to ensure a peaceful succession. In spite of these precautions, it was not often that an emperor succeeded to the throne without having to fight one or other of his brothers, aided by his adversary's maternal family. The nobility, so completely submissive to the will of the emperor during his reign, played an important part in the politics of the interregnum and, by putting its weight on one şide or the other, influenced the fate of the empire.

The duty of arranging a worthy funeral for the Inca fell to his *ayllu*. The dead man was followed to his tomb by a number of his women and servants, either voluntarily or because they were forced to do so. In the course of these funeral rites and the dances that followed them, the victims chosen to accompany the dead man were made drunk with *chicha* and strangled. When the Spaniards were conducting the funeral service of Atahuallpa, whom they had strangled in the square at Cajamarca, the ceremony was interrupted by the cries of his wives, who, all disheveled, burst into the chapel to kill themselves on the body of their husband. In spite of everything the Spaniards did to dissuade them from this "horrible decision," many of them committed suicide that very evening.

The viscera were drawn from the corpse through a cut in the abdomen, and the body embalmed with balsams and dried in the sun, or in some other way. To give the body some semblance of life, false eyes were made from thin plates of gold, and pieces of calabash were put in the cheeks. The body was dressed in sumptuous clothes and wrapped in cotton. In 1560, Garcilaso de la Vega had occasion to see the mummies of five Incas found by Polo de Ondegardo after a long search. Not a hair of their heads was missing, nor a single eyebrow hair; their arms were crossed over the stomach and their eyes turned downward. When he touched the hand of Huayna Capac "it seemed as hard as wood." "Moreover," he adds, "these bodies weighed so little that the smallest Indian could carry one in his arms or on his shoulders." When these mummies were carried along the streets "everyone knelt down and adored them with tears in his eyes. The Spaniards even took off their hats because these had once been the bodies of kings, and this gave enormous pleasure to the Indians."

The mummy of each Inca was kept in the palace he had had built, though some authors maintain they were placed on seats in the big hall of the Temple of the Sun.

Indian agricultural workers and shepherds were given the task of serving the dead emperors. It was the duty of the *panaka*, that is, the line springing from the sovereign, to watch over his body and to see it was worshipped. The mission of the ministers attached to his person was to divine what he wanted. Sometimes they decided the mummy desired to eat and drink, at others that it wanted to visit another mummy. On each occasion there would be a festival. The dead Incas also went on visits to the living in their houses.

The lands belonging to the royal mummies became so extensive that Huáscar, at the start of his short reign, decided to dispossess them to stop the encroachment of the dead upon the living. This wise step brought him the enmity of the royal lines, who found these properties profitable.

During his lifetime the Inca was sacred and semidivine, and after his death he became a god almost equal to the greatest gods of the empire: the Creator, the Sun, the God of Thunder, and the Moon Goddess. Every time the statues and symbols of the gods were shown in the great square at Cuzco, the Inca mummies were also brought out, each in its litter, and put on stools in proper order around the square, for the sovereigns of Hanan Cuzco, from the upper part of the town, were separated from those of Hurin Cuzco, in the lower part. Each mummy was sur-

House of the dead, Marañon

rounded by priests, servants, and women entrusted with driving away the flies.

All those in any way descended from the founder of the empire, Manco Capac, had the right to the title of Inca, and to participate to some extent in the authority and prestige of the emperor. At Cuzco, in the mid-sixteenth century, there were eleven royal *ayllus*. Each of these lines, or *panakas,* had as ancestor one of the legendary or historic sovereigns of the dynasty. Indeed it was the custom that one of the Inca's sons, other than the heir presumptive, "had the task of protecting all the other sons and relations, and these recognized him as chief for all their needs and took his name." (Sarmiento) The members of each *ayllu* kept alive the worship of their common ancestor and looked after

88

his mummy and the sacred articles that had belonged to him, or were reputed to have been his. The royal lines were not enough to supply all the crown officers needed to administer the ever extending territory, consequently the emperor gave the *ayllus* between the Vilcanota valley and Abancay the right to the title Inca. The groups which, as a result of conquest or alliances, had fused their destiny with that of the Incas were called "Incas by privilege."

A good part of the tribute the provinces sent to Cuzco fell to the share of this aristocracy. The riches displayed by the nobles that contributed so much to the pomp of the court had another source besides the clothes, jewels, and women the emperor gave as a reward for some service or for friendship's sake. Many of the nobles had posts which made them veritable satraps, and even those who had no very spectacular position enjoyed rights that gave them an economically privileged status. The members of the royal line were allowed to wear some of the Inca insignia, though different from the Inca's in detail; thus their ear disks were smaller and their *llautus,* headbands, of a single color, whereas that of the Inca was in four colors.

On reaching puberty, young aristocrats went through certain initiation rites which distinguished them from their subjects, who experienced no ceremony of importance at this stage. The Spaniards were always looking for parallels between the Inca and their own civilization, and saw this as identical to the ceremonies preceding admission to the orders of chivalry. To some extent they were right, for the ceremonies and ordeals performed in both cases gave the young man's privileged position a social and religious sanction.

The initiation ceremony was called *huarachicoy,* from *huara,* the loincloth that was solemnly given to the initiates at the end of the ritual. The ceremony included a number of purely religious rites, such as sacrifices to the *huaca,* processions, and dances before the idols, alternating with tests of a symbolic or magical nature, such as beatings, races, and trials of courage and endurance. One would have to be very naive, like Baudin, to turn the *huarachicoy* into "a kind of examination ending in a course of instruction." We are dealing here with extremely ancient ceremonies such as are still in use among some Brazilian tribes (the

Apinayé, Cayapo, and Sherente), when the young men pass from one age group to another. The very full details supplied by the old writers on the subject of these initiation ceremonies need not detain us here, except those that show the wish to exalt the glory of the empire and endow the young men with pride in their caste and fidelity to their lord, the Inca.

The novices, during a short period of seclusion, had to listen to distinguished warriors recounting the exploits of their ancestors and exhorting them to follow in the footsteps of their worthy predecessors. As they climbed to the Huanacauri *huaca,* they were preceded by the imperial mascot and the badges of sovereignty, the banner and the *suntur paukar,* or feathered lance. This climb was the culminating ceremony of the initiation. The slings with which they were beaten symbolized those carried by the ancestors when they came out of their cave of Tampu-Tocco. The oldest members of their families reminded them from time to time that "they should not neglect the service of the Inca under pain of punishment." These elders also explained "the far-off origin of the ceremony" and recalled to them "the victories and good deeds of the Incas and of their ancestors."

After being given arms by the "principal uncle" and a final beating, the young men were enjoined by their relatives "to show themselves brave and loyal and to respect the gods."

The initiation ended with the piercing of the ears, an operation effected, in certain cases at least, by the Inca himself, using little gold rods which were left in the hole. By progressively introducing larger plugs the "knights" were able gradually to enlarge the earlobe to a bigger and bigger size till finally they could wear the big ear disks that led the Spaniards to call them *orejones* (big-eared ones).

of the Empire

The myth of the great Inca socialist state springs from a merely cursory aquaintance with its institutions. The property laws particularly, as well as the subject's duties to the emperor, have been interpreted in terms of European ideas, which apply only very imperfectly to a civilization still, in many respects, archaic despite its complexity and refinement.

The Inca economic and social system, as described by Garcilaso de la Vega in his *Royal Commentaries,* and by those writers whom he inspired, had a fine and admirable simplicity: the sovereigns of old Peru wanted justice and prosperity to spread through the land, and as soon as a province was conquered, it was "divided into three parts, the first for the Sun, the second for the king, and the third for the people."

The fields of the Sun God were cultivated to supply the needs of the religion and to maintain the numerous priesthood. The Inca's land was cultivated for the benefit of the government, and could also be used as an emergency fund when some calamity over-

Doorway to an Inca courtyard

took one province or another. Finally, the last third of arable land, divided annually into equal portions, was distributed to the families of each community, in proportion to their numbers. A commoner's possessions amounted to no more than his hut, a yard, a few domestic animals, and household goods such as clothes and tools. Everything else belonged to the Inca. The inhabitants of the empire worked for the Inca, who, in exchange, left them free to dispose of the communal land as they wished, and also gave them a fair share of the fruits of their labor. If such was indeed the economic framework of the Inca state, one could truly speak of state socialism grafted onto agrarian collectivism. But was it really like this?

In fact, the Inca empire combined absolute despotism with a respect for the social and political forms of the subject peoples. The Inca reigned as absolute monarch, but his will reached the common man only through the local chiefs, whose authority and privileges were maintained, if not reinforced. Centralization of power was combined, after a fashion, with the exercise of indirect rule, if such an anachronistic phrase may be allowed.

The most unusual aspects of Inca civilization—the tripartite division of land, the convents of the "Virgins of the Sun," the state storehouses, the statistics, and the road network—reflect a very special concept of the subject's obligations toward his sovereign, and a very ingenious organization of the country's resources in man and materials, secured by a ruthless imperialist policy within less than a century.

Inca society did not practice slavery, at least in the usual interpretation of the word. It is only very late that we find the emperor and his governors tearing people from their homes and settling them on their own estates. Tributes could not be paid in money, since its use was not known, even in the primitive form developed in Mexico and Colombia. Gold and silver were thought of only as raw materials for the purpose of making ornaments or religious objects. The Incas would certainly have been able to pre-empt part of each village's crops, but they preferred to draw on a far richer tribute, the work and energy of their people. The Incas, as local country chieftains, had had a right to the *corvée* and to the personal services of the peasants. Being masters of a great empire, they maintained the right to press the inhabitants into their service on a vast scale and to their own profit, as they had done in former times on a smaller scale.

The *corvée* system became so important in the economic life of the empire that, even at the height of its power, "tributes," that is taxes, were all paid in personal services, and no Indian was taxed on his goods. The notion of compulsory service was so deeply ingrained in the Indians' mentality that, as the Spaniards found with considerable surprise, an Indian would prefer forced labor, even of two weeks' duration, "rather than give the authorities so much as a bushel of potatoes."

As soon as a province was conquered, the first task of the Inca's officers was to evaluate the resources of the area in men and crops. On the basis of this information, the Inca proceeded to mark out the lands that would fall to the state, and those that would go to the religion of the Sun and the principal official divinities.

In taking a part of the conquered people's land, the Incas changed the existing landowning system, but the change was not fundamental. It would be slanted to their own advantage and to the advantage of their own titular gods: the structure was not altered, the *ayllus* did not lose their communes, even if a part were confiscated, nor did the *huacas* and the *curacas* lose their properties. The changes introduced by the imperial officers resulted in the incorporation of the Inca into each conquered territory, since the Incas were content merely to claim for themselves and their gods the rights and privileges previously given from time immemorial to the *ayllus* and idols of the region. Looked at in this way, it was not so much a question of the community adapting itself to new conditions as the dynasty of the Incas, to some extent, identifying itself with the old order and taking root in the community. The whole weight of this new distribution of land, and of the new personal services demanded, fell on the peasants who now, in addition to their obligations to their old chiefs and traditional gods, had to cultivate the fields of the Inca and those of the new gods.

What were the proportions of the Inca's and the Sun's lands to those left to the community? Once again our sources are vague and even contradictory on this point. According to Polo de Ondegardo, considered an authority on this matter, the Inca took the lion's share but saw that the community was left with enough

94

to live on. A valuable sixteenth-century document informs us that in the Chincha valley, on the coast of Peru, every thousand households were forced to give the Cuzco sovereign lands which varied in area according to the nature of the soil, but usually averaged about fifteen acres. In reality these expropriations were not always from the arable land. The conquerors were often content to accept part of the wasteland, which they made productive by irrigation and terracing. We must remember that the Incas favored the growing of maize, and the admirable terraced hills they formed on the slopes of the valleys were designed for that purpose.

The lands set aside for maintaining the religion were relatively large, whether taken from one tenant or several, even if the area was not as big as the Inca's share. Polo de Ondegardo goes so far as to say that he thinks there is no nation in the world that "spends so much in sacrifices and devotes so much land to this end." It is true that these "gods' acres" did not all belong to the Sun God, for the sanctuaries and local gods kept the fields they owned before the conquest.

The soil needed to be rich indeed to support such demands; the confiscations were bitterly resented by the subject peoples. They did not forget their lost lands, and had no hesitation in reclaiming them from the Spaniards after the fall of the Incas.

It seems unlikely that the Incas tried to interfere in local affairs or attempted to control the amount of land going to each family. Local usages were respected. Whether the land was distributed annually or not, the community certainly took notice of each family's needs, "although they never received more than was necessary for their subsistence, even if there was additional land available."

As there were no day laborers or slaves, the area of land a family could use effectively was proportional to its numbers. In certain *ayllus* the fields were cultivated in turn by the whole community; in others, only relatives helped each other.

The empire's land system, then, was characterized by the contrast between the communal lands and those belonging to the Inca and to the Sun. However, private sequestration of the soil was not unknown. Private property was acquired through gifts made by the Inca to those nobles enjoying his friendship, or to those whom he wished to reward for service in time of war or for great

Machu Picchu

works undertaken for the public good. This type of generosity was also extended to the priests and the royal concubines sent back to their own countries. The lands bestowed by the Inca could not be taken away or taxed. On the death of the owner they passed to the beneficiary's heirs, who were expected to cultivate them in common and make an equal distribution of the produce. The amount of produce going to each household was equal, but anyone who failed to do his share of the sowing lost the right to his portion of the crop. Were these royal gifts made at the community's expense, or were they taken from the royal property? It is still in doubt. The lands the Inca distributed could probably be taken either from the *ayllus* or from his own estate; there is no text extant which enables us to answer the question. Doubtless there was no fixed rule on the subject, and decisions on this point were dictated by the particular circumstances and the situation of the gift land.

The nobleman or civil servant who received a gift of property did not on that account lose his rights in his *ayllu*'s common lands. The Inca's favor was thus the origin of a new type of property grafted onto the old system.

On the outskirts of Cuzco, notably in the fertile Yucay valley, the Incas had big private estates, which remained theirs even after death since they served for the support of their mummies and the domestic staff that cared for them. We do not know by what means the Incas had succeeded in appropriating the best land in the Cuzco region. Doubtless they had no qualms about arbitrary confiscation; Pachacuti turned out all the Indians in a radius of five leagues around the capital and distributed their lands to members of the imperial family.

The Incas attacked the territorial integrity of communities, not only by taking a third for themselves and another for their gods, but by the outright confiscation of all the land of rebel areas. Many such punitive confiscations date from the reign of the last great emperor, Huayna Capac, at the beginning of the sixteenth century. The lands taken from their legitimate owners fell to the Inca or were given to his favorites.

Did the *Sapa Inca* have a pre-emptive right to all the empire's lands or only to the wasteland, pasture, and forest? This question has often been debated, but it seems a little pointless when we are dealing with an absolute sovereign disposing of the life and property of his subjects as he wished. Communities might profit from exploiting the natural resources of their area, always provided it did not harm the interests of the ruling class. The gold and silver mines and the gold-bearing rivers no doubt belonged to the Inca, though certain local chiefs, or even communities, seem to have exploited them to their advantage. Nevertheless, they were obliged to send part of the metal as tribute to Cuzco. The coca plantations in the hot valleys belonged to the Inca. They were cultivated by his own men, often Indians guilty of some offense, for work in the unhealthy subtropical valleys was considered a punishment.

The Indians did not have the right to hunt game on their land, this pleasure being reserved for the Inca and his nobles. From time to time immense hunts, called *chacu,* were organized, using veritable armies of peasants, in the course of which thousands of animals were slaughtered.

The Incas claimed a large part of the flocks of llamas and alpacas, which were the wealth of the inhabitants of the highlands. Only the animals consecrated to the religion were as numerous as those of the Inca. Shepherd communities had only small numbers as their own property. Heads of families had the right to only about a dozen beasts in all. According to the services he gave, or the favor in which he stood, the *curaca* received a greater or lesser number of beasts as a present.

The communal flock was shorn at the appropriate time and the wool distributed to the villagers, each receiving the amount fitted to his condition, his needs, and those of his wife and children. Inspections were made to see if they had spun the wool and made clothes, and those who had been neglectful were punished.

All the members of an *ayllu* received the same amount, even those who, owning a flock of llamas, could have done without, which proves that the family rights could not be prescribed, even though this made for inequality among them.

The wool from the state flocks was spun and woven by the community, who made cloth and garments for the sovereign and for the sacrifices, "for large quantities of the *kumbi* quality (that is, the best) were burned."

The Incas, as owners of part of the land, naturally had to look to collective cultivation of the land by the community. Without peasant manpower, the lands brought into their estate would be valueless. The emperor's *corvée* was imposed on every married man. All labor dues for the state were carried out by the *hatun-runa,* that is, the "adults," only married men being considered as such. It was thus in the state's interest to see that the young men did not delay too long in getting married and establishing a household, or take advantage of their celibacy to avoid their obligations. Possibly this explains the more or less regular visits of inspectors to the villages, when they called together the young men and women who ought to be united in marriage by their authority. These officials no doubt ratified decisions already taken by the interested parties themselves, or by their families. It does not seem that they enforced any arbitrary decision or that they went against individual likings, unless there was rivalry for the hand of a young woman. In such a case they would interfere only as an arbiter or judge. After this official betrothal the official wedding took place, celebrated according to the customs of each region. It was not easy to get rid of a wife who had been bestowed in marriage by the Inca or his representative. Monogamy was the rule for the common man. Only the Inca caste and the imperial officials had the right to several wives, polygamy being a status symbol, a symbol of rank and prestige.

From the point of view of the state the household, not the individual, was the basic economic unit. Though young people, the aged, and women were not counted when tasks were given out, they nonetheless took part, as far as their strength permitted, in the work in the fields. Each household liable to service had to till a section of the Inca's field, or the Sun's. "He who is assisted by a large family and finishes the task before the others is called a rich man." Work on the Inca's and the Sun's fields was thus a periodic duty, whose length varied from region to region. The order in which the field work was done, according to different types of soil, has given rise to contrary assertions. Garcilaso de la Vega, in a much quoted passage, asserts that the peasants started with the Sun's fields, then went to those of the widows and orphans, and of soldiers away at the wars, ending with those of the *curaca* and the Inca. Other texts of a less apologist nature inform us that the Inca had priority. The produce from the Inca's and the Sun's fields was stored in granaries situated along the roads or in easily accessible places. Part of it was sent to Cuzco, to serve the needs of the sovereign and the noble families. The remainder was used for the officials, the army, and the gangs of government workers. Finally, supplies could be drawn from these granaries to feed the population in case of a crop failure.

Dependent peasants were formed into gangs, not only to till the fields of the poor and the infirm but, in addition, those of families whose head was serving in the army or the Inca's gangs. Lastly, the rural community repaired the roads and saw to the proper working of the irrigation system.

Tribute was also levied in the form of *mita,* forced labor, when the Inca or local governors had special need of abundant manpower. In this way war was comparable to labor service for the state. The guarding and supplying of the resthouses, *tambos*, along the imperial roads fell to the local communities, as did the responsibility for the provision of two relay runners at the post house always ready to carry a message. In the stock-raising areas, the *ayllus* had to take care of the Inca's and the Sun's flocks. They no doubt appointed the shepherds who took turns to carry out these duties.

Women were not subject to labor service or tax, but in practice they did not escape it since a part of the field work fell to them and they spun the thread and wove the cloth taken by the state for its stores. Sometimes they accompanied their husbands to the wars, carrying provisions and preparing the food.

The villages supplied servants for the chiefs or the Inca's court, and were obliged, in addition, to bring before an Inca official all the young girls from eight to ten years old. The prettiest were sent to a "convent," where, under the control of an elderly woman, they carried out various tasks, in particular the making of fine cloth from vicuña wool. They were again inspected at the age of puberty. The most beautiful were reserved for the Inca's harem or given as concubines to the nobles or important officials. The others were put to serve in a temple and became the priestesses' servants. Finally, a few were set aside for human sacrifice.

The peasants who cultivated the fields belonging to the Inca and the Sun, as well as those employed on public works, received their food free from the state granaries for the duration of the work. It was the same for the soldiers, "who left for war supplied with food, arms, shoes, and clothes all coming from the Inca's depots; they lacked for nothing." What has often been interpreted as an example of Inca paternalism is no more than the application, on a governmental scale, of the rural tradition of helping one another, as strong today as it was four hundred years ago: the individual who benefits from the help of his neighbors is willing to supply their wants as long as they put themselves out for him. Custom requires that he should be generous and make quite a celebration of the work from which he will profit. The compulsory work for the Inca can alone be considered, to some extent, as mutual aid among the peasantry. It was also carried out with songs and dances and a cheerful atmosphere which the Spaniards,

An aryballus

quite mistakenly, saw as the result of wise measures taken to keep the people contented.

Among a community's obligations to the Inca was the supply of various handicrafts. Each household had to deliver to the tax collector a certain quantity of articles it had made: stuffs, clothes,

Old skills are not forgotten

shoes, rope. The raw materials came from regional depots. Time
and trouble were the sole contribution of statute laborers. The
wealth and luxury of the Incas, a subject which never ceases to
be commented upon in the accounts of the conquests, as well as
the high technical and artistic qualities of the exhibits in our
museums, presuppose numerous craftsmen—jewelers, weavers,
potters, and sculptors. While a large part of the everyday articles
were made at home by the peasants, the luxury goods—fine cloth,
jewelry, ceramics—were the work of specialists. Some craftsmen
worked directly for the court, while others were stationed in the
workshops of provincial governors or local princes. Custom de-

creed that royal officials who came to see the Inca should give him a valuable present. They could not have done so without skilled workmen available to make the objects. These workmen and artists, separated from all links with their villages, were fed and clothed at the Inca's expense, or at the expense of some dignitary who employed them, and were exempt from labor service. The "Virgins of the Sun," who wove fine, richly embroidered cloth from vicuña wool, could be likened to the craftsmen in their workshops. The situation of these people, who spent all their lives working for the court or for an important dignitary, resembled that of the craftsmen of ancient Egypt who, at whim of the Pharaoh, were attached to the person of a "nomarch."

The position of these artisans shows no essential difference from that of the *yanas,* a category of persons with a somewhat ill-defined and often contradictory status, seeming at some times to be veritable slaves and at others privileged officials. These *yanas,* having been torn from their communities, were entirely dependent on those they served. Some had been captured in the wars; others were criminals or relatives of criminals who, as a result of the system of collective responsibility, had been reduced to this condition. However, the majority of the *yanas* were young people given by the rural communities to the Inca or his representative as servants. Many of them became manservants, bodyguards, or the Inca's litter bearers. Others fulfilled the same tasks for provincial governors or helped in their administration. Some of them even became important, thanks to their intimacy with the powerful. Some received women as a reward for their zeal in serving the master, others were given more *yanas* as servants. Unfortunately we know very little of these parvenus. It is nonetheless significant that the Inca's favor, or that of one of his·dignitaries, could make a person of humble origin important. It is wrong to neglect this side of Inca society, which hardly tallies with the theory of their society so often put forward. In this respect, as in many others, the so-called socialist state looks very like an Asiatic type of monarchy.

Privileged *yanas* were the exception. The majority were attached to the private estates of the Inca or the aristocrats in the same way as the *colonos* are to the haciendas of modern Peru. The growing importance of the *yanas* as the empire expanded

Tunic, Inca period

can only be explained if their production was greater than that obtained by the traditional system of labor service. In removing part of the people from a community the Incas weakened it and sowed the seeds of a revolution which, had they grown, would have changed the structure of the empire. From a group of mainly autonomous agricultural collectives it would have become a species of "prefeudal empire," with huge estates, owned by nobles and officials, being worked by serfs or even slaves.

The taxes in kind which accumulated in the Inca's storehouses were used for many purposes. Some of this produce was sent to Cuzco, but most of it was used locally to support the officials, the army, and the gangs employed on state projects. There is no doubt that these stores were drawn on to feed the local population if crops failed and famine threatened.

In an agricultural and craft-based state, where the government restricted the movement of population and goods, and where all surpluses were sent to public storehouses by government order, one might suppose that trading, under the best of conditions, cannot have been anything more than bartering. But once again, in fact, it is not as simple as that. It is true that the Inca, or his governors, could regulate interregional exchanges just as they wished. If the crop was insufficient in one province, the Inca sent in supplies from a region where it was abundant; foodstuffs that could not be grown in a certain zone, because of the climate, were regularly imported on a barter basis; finally, luxury goods made by the Inca's craftsmen were redistributed in the shape of gifts. The market controllers sometimes sought to get products in short supply in the empire from the unconquered peoples beyond the frontiers. It was no doubt by means of a regular barter trade with the Amazon forest Indians that the Incas obtained the tropical feathers with which they adorned themselves, as well as resins and medicinal plants.

To deduce from the above that the state had a trading monopoly would be both a misuse of language and an anachronism. In a mountainous country like Peru, where short distances often separate very different geographical zones, the barter of certain products was perfectly logical. Even before the Inca period the people from the cold regions would penetrate into the semi-tropical valleys with the object of getting at least some variety in their food. The Peruvian markets have grown since the use of money was adopted, but they are no novelty introduced by the Spaniards. In 1532, Estete was struck by the bustle at the Jauja fair, and there was an important market at Cuzco. No doubt trading was done only by means of barter and the market served only limited areas. Each family owned the products from its own land and could dispose of the animals it had raised. Certain raw materials essential for the craftsmen and technicians must also have been traded.

The commerce of the empire, limited though it was, was not merely barter between neighboring localities. It appears, though there is no definite proof, that there were a number of real merchants who traveled long distances to trade in certain products. It is true that this class of persons was not numerous and that the references to them are rare. But if commerce was a state monopoly, how does one explain the tolls levied at bridgeheads, noted by the Spaniards when they first came into the empire? At Cajas the guards extracted a toll in kind from those who came and went, "for nobody could leave the town with a bundle unless he paid a tax." This old custom was abolished by Atahuallpa, at least for produce going to the army. No one might leave the town, under pain of death, except by a road on which a guard was posted.

The emperor Pachacuti had even ordered that there should be merchants, and if the people trading in raw materials such as gold, silver, and precious stones were strictly supervised, it was not so much to restrict their business as to discover whence came the produce they carried. Does not the capture, by Pizarro's pilot Bartolomé Ruiz, of an immense raft loaded with goods, prove that the coastal peoples had not abandoned commerce, in spite of their subjugation by the Incas? Finally, the abundance of pure Inca-style objects found from Ecuador to Chile suggests the survival of old trading customs which the Incas did not try to destroy in order to retain their so-called monopoly. However, archaeologists maintain that exchanges between the coast and the interior were more numerous in the Tiahuanaco period than during the Inca dynasty.

By virtue of this system, the empire's communities were self-sufficient and produced a surplus, thanks to which the nobles and officials lived a life of ease, or even of luxury. This surplus was so big that veritable armies of workers could be maintained to build the enormous Inca structures and to carry on wars against innumerable people, and the artisans could be paid. Part of the taxes collected by the Inca was regularly redistributed in the form of presents to the court nobles, to the more zealous officials, and to local chiefs and princes whose fidelity and devotion had to be ensured. Such generosity, carried out on a large scale and sanctified by custom, has led people to believe there was an Incaic "Welfare State." In fact the Inca was merely behaving as a chief, behavior common in many archaic societies, particularly in America. He who commands must be generous, for if not, he risks losing the support of his men. The Indian cacique, like a good father, sees to it that no one is hungry or naked, even if it means he himself must make sacrifices.

The immense size of the buildings constructed by the Incas, their cyclopean magnificence, the daring roads over the mountains, and the huge agricultural terraces have led us to greatly admire the sovereigns who ordered such works, but we should not forget the toil of the workmen engaged in their construction. Most of the chroniclers praise the spirit of justice in which work was distributed. It seems in fact that the number of peasants engaged in labor service was small compared to the rest of the population. It has been conjectured that to construct the fortress of Sacsahuamán, the largest Inca building, required a labor force of 30,000 men. If we assume that the population of the empire was eight million, then this represented not more than 1.9 percent of those eligible for labor service—that is adult men between twenty and fifty years old—and even if we assume the population to have been only four million, these 30,000 are still only 3.8 percent.

The administrative system of the Incas seems to have been designed mainly to secure the easy working of the different *corvées*, whether the aims were to provide for the ruling class, public works, or war. A Spanish official saw it in this way:

The government of the Incas suits them very well, for they have liberty in practically nothing. They have plenty of superiors and chiefs set over them, making them work, till the fields, sow, weave, and do other tasks, so that they can pay their taxes. If the Indians were just left alone, if the caciques were not after them all the time, they would give way to idleness and do no work with which to pay their tax.

The Inca's authority stretched through a complete hierarchy of officials which ran from viziers, chosen from among his closest associates, down to humble foremen in charge of a gang of five persons.

The use of such enormous resources of men and materials

would hardly be possible without constant counting and recording. The Inca had to be constantly advised as to the number of soldiers or workers the provinces could supply, and the number of young girls who could be sent to the temples or given to officers and officials. The first population census was made by Topa Yupanqui, who came to the throne in 1471.

The *tukrikuks,* or governors, were bidden to collect this statistical information and to give it to the Inca at the feast of *Inti-raymi*. The census takers were special officials, the *quipu-kamayocs,* who registered the count on knotted cords; different colors correspond to different classes of persons or things. As there was no registry of births, marriages, and deaths, and no one could give his exact age, the population was divided into ten categories, according to apparent age and ability to work. Children able to help their parents were in a different class from those yet too young to work, and another category included those too infirm to undertake any work.

This preoccupation with statistics has been advanced as a proof of the socialist nature of the Inca empire. But we must beware of being taken in by words. The numbering of the population by age groups and the measuring of the wealth produced by forced labor were done to serve very simple ends. The Incas could never have undertaken their conquests, nor have built the numerous fortresses and palaces, unless they had known the size of the labor force to be drawn on and the amount of produce available to maintain them. The use of the knotted cords, based on the decimal system, no doubt led the Incas to divide the population of the empire according to this same system.

The entire male population between the ages of twenty-five and about forty was divided into groups of 10, 100, 500, 1,000, and 10,000 souls, for the greater convenience of the census officials. Each group was placed under the authority of an official whose rank and prestige depended on the number of individuals he commanded. The provincial governor was the head of this hierarchy, and was nominated by the Inca; in theory the governor had authority over about 40,000 tributary households, or say 200,000 people, if we reckon five people to each family, whose chief had to pay tribute and give labor service. These administrative units were supposed to correspond to lineages, *ayllus,* of

Accountant with his quipu

tribes and of the old provinces. The *pachaca,* a hundred families, for example, was the synonym for an *ayllu.* No one has yet succeeded in explaining how this rigid decimal classification could be adapted to the traditional social structures. It is difficult to believe that such an adaptation is anything other than a bureaucratic fiction or some crude approximation, whose sole advantage was to facilitate the counting of potential soldiers and workers in any given region. One must not, however, entirely neglect the evidence of the chroniclers, who stress the efforts made by the Inca officials to get into new groups of ten any surplus of people from the old groups. This tendency to count in bulk, rather than in units, is by no means confined to the Incas.

There is a suggestion that the Inca administration was one built by theoreticians obsessed with the ideas of symmetry and logic. But such abstract theorizing tempts us to forget that the empire was made up of different states, confederations, rural communities, and tribes, all keeping their own individuality, traditions, and leaders. Over this very mixed world the Inca ruled by means of officials recruited from the royal *ayllu,* the most influential of which were his nearest relations. The empire was divided into four regions, or quarters: *Chincha-suyu, Cunti-suyu, Colla-suyu,* and *Anti-suyu,* each having a chief, or *apo,* at its head, generally a person of high rank, a brother or an uncle of the Inca. These *apos* were likened by the Spaniards to viceroys, and formed a kind of council to help the sovereign. However, the chief duty of an *apo* was to attend to local affairs and to discuss them with his colleagues. All important decisions came from the Inca himself.

The provinces, whose territory corresponded more or less to that of the former state or tribes now part of the empire, were administered by the *tukrikuks,* governors, once again members of the imperial *ayllu.* They lived in the provincial capital, generally a town founded by the Inca and bearing the name of the province with the prefix *hatun*—big. Officials below the rank of *tukrikuk* did not have to be of the Inca caste. The innumerable *curacas,* some of whom were powerful lords, were local chieftains whose importance in the administrative hierarchy depended on the number of families under their jurisdiction.

Curacas of a certain rank, generally chiefs ruling ten thousand families, as well as governors appointed by the Inca, had to go to

Cuzco every May, present themselves at court, and give an account of their stewardship. These visits coincided with the delivery of tribute, and it is probable that certain officials accompanied the Indian porters carrying it to the capital. As a sign of homage, the *curacas* had to deliver gold dust, silver ore, or pieces of jewelry. This was the moment that the Inca listened to any complaints against his officials, and decided the fate of the accused.

After having distributed part of the tribute received to members of his family, and to those who had served him well and "made themselves agreeable," he gave out

women, servants, agricultural land, or beautiful clothes made from fine-woven cloth. The *curacas* might also be allowed the distinction of being carried in a litter or hammock, *yanas* being supplied as bearers. They were, in addition, permitted to use a parasol, to sit on a stool, or to use a gold or silver service for their food, a much prized concession, for no one dared do so without the Inca's permission.

These gifts were all the more appreciated since the Inca saw to it that

those who came from Collao should receive goods brought from the Andes, and to those who came from Cunti-suyu he gave articles from other regions, such things as were lacking in their own countries. That which had been given to him he gave to others, so much so that the greater part of what had been brought was used up, and with these gifts he welcomed them and made merry with them. Those who deserved chastisement were severely punished and the others were sent home with kindness. (*Discurso de la sucesión y gobierno de los Incas*)

Sons of the *curacas* who were destined to succeed their fathers were obliged to stay at court. They were in effect hostages for the loyalty of their fathers, but at the same time they absorbed Inca civilization and learned the workings of the administrative system; it was a nursery for future *curacas* and officials, trained to become the useful tools of the imperial policy. The Pharaohs, and later the Caesars, behaved in the same way when they gave an Egyptian or Roman education to the sons of the barbarian kings and chiefs.

At the death of a *curaca*, the heir came to power only if the Inca knew him personally and invested the powers in him. Regional chiefs were also represented at court by a kind of ambassador, who kept the sovereign informed of what went on in their masters' territories.

However perfect such a hierarchical, decimal-based system may appear, it seemed to inspire the Inca with only a limited confidence in its efficiency, since he sought, in addition, to exert a direct control over his governors and local *curacas*. At more or less regular intervals, or when circumstances warranted it, the Inca sent out *tokoyrikoks*, "those who see all," veritable *missi dominici,* as inspectors of the provinces, to see that the taxes were paid and that the contingents of soldiers or workers he had ordered were raised. The "king's eyes" nearly always belonged to the Inca caste, and received an insignia from him bearing witness to the official nature of the duties performed. As they represented the emperor, they were fed and lodged by the local authorities. Wherever they stopped, they inquired into the conduct of different officials, and sought information on crimes committed in the region. Their reports often led to the dispatch of special judges, charged with the punishment of the offenders.

When the Inca visited a province, he automatically assumed full powers there. He made decisions, not only on the public works to be carried out, but also on any punishments to be administered. On their side, the governors also appointed their own subordinates if they thought it necessary. Following their master's example, they surrounded themselves with councilors and servants they trusted completely, and to whom they delegated some of their powers as soon as they feared they might be disobeyed, or only halfheartedly obeyed, by the lower orders. Thus the administrative structure of the empire was characterized by the existence of two systems of control: a series of hierarchial groups, and a parallel direct control under the command of agents and dignitaries appointed by the king. Consequently, with the Incas, as in many other totalitarian states, there existed a bureaucracy itself subject to constant supervision.

The officials' duties were vaguely defined and stretched over the widest field. Apart from the *quipu-kamayocs,* comparable to the Egyptian scribes, they were in no way specialists. According to need, they became tax collectors, generals, engineers, lawmakers, chiefs of police, and above all judges. The range of activities narrowed as it approached the lower ranks; the decurions were hardly more than foremen.

Justice was administered according to the customary law of each province, for, contrary to what the chroniclers say, it is hardly likely that the Incas would have imposed a uniform code of laws on all their peoples, except in matters affecting the imperial authority. Any action against the Inca's power or authority was severely punished. Rebellion, attempts at rebellion, or even the suspicion of trying to bewitch the emperor, refusal to pay taxes, or a theft to the detriment of the state were all major crimes that were the province of special judges appointed by the Inca, and were punishable by death preceded by torture.

To seduce a Virgin of the Sun was also held to be an attack on the Inca's majesty. When Pizarro and his men reached Cajas they saw "a building occupied by five hundred women doing nothing else but spinning and making maize wine"; outside were the bodies of a number of men hung up by the feet. On asking what crimes these poor wretches had committed, Pizarro was told "a man had succeeded in approaching one of these women and had been put to death, along with the guards who had allowed it to happen."

The village chief punished minor offenses, and like a justice of the peace tried to maintain good feeling among the families. He had to arbitrate over boundary disputes and settle quarrels over water rights. Theft, on the other hand, was a serious crime; those guilty of it, unless they had stolen from necessity, were beaten with a stone, and put to death in the case of a second offense, if the provincial governor confirmed the sentence.

All the sentences given and carried out had to be reported by the judges to their superiors in the hierarchy, and by means of the administrative network the Inca, in theory, ended up by being informed of the principal crimes committed even in his most distant provinces.

The actual trial procedure used in the empire is not well known. The trial was carried out in the presence of all those from far and near who were in any way affected by the case. Torture was used to obtain confessions, and if this failed, they resorted to divination. The guilty party was beaten on the back with a large stone.

One of the Inca's most effective methods of consolidating his empire was the movement of population; such displacements were frequent and on a vast scale. If the inhabitants of a recently conquered region seemed rebellious, or gave some cause for alarm, the Inca would establish a colony of known loyal subjects among them. The natives had to provide for the newcomers for two years, and the state storehouses also were at their disposal, until, having built their villages and brought their fields into cultivation, they had achieved economic independence. These colonists, *mitimaes*, wore their national dress and spoke their own language and were under the authority of the governor.

Although they cannot really be likened to military garrisons, at times they carried out similar surveillance duties. It has been said that in order to nip in the bud any conspiracy growing in the dark, they had the right to spy on the natives, even in their houses. Once the *mitimaes* were established in their new surroundings and were self-sufficient, they became almost an army of occupation which cost the state nothing and did not oppress the conquered.

In some cases a whole troublesome population would be deported to some part of the empire where the Inca's rule was undisputed. The exiles, whether rebels or loyal subjects, left the homes they would never see again, taking their household goods with them. Terrible punishment was meted out to those who succumbed to the temptation of returning home.

The importance assumed by these deportations is clear from the constant reference made by the Spanish officials to the *mitimaes* in the descriptions they left of the areas coming under their control. Questions were constantly coming up in connection with Indian villages established by one of the victorious Incas. During the colonial period these settlers demanded different treatment to that meted out to the natives. Even today communities can still be found whose inhabitants claim to be descendants of *mitimaes* from central Peru.

These massive deportations have been interpreted as the realization of a systematic plan to make the whole empire one homogeneous body. The *mitimaes* would thus have been the instruments of this policy of assimilation. But the pains taken by the new arrivals to differentiate themselves from the native population, and the privileged position given to those led by the *orejones,* that is, by members of the royal line who came from the heart of the empire, contradict any such notion.

The Inca state has been so much extolled in the past that it is not surprising that a reaction in the opposite direction has taken place. If, at one time, it was the fashion to praise an administration powerful enough to have introduced standard practices everywhere, today we tend to emphasize local differences and the persistence of regional customs and social structures. Inca despotism seems more theoretical than real, and now the tendency is to doubt the efficacy of its control over the population. The truth no doubt lies somewhere between these two extremes. The Tahuantin-suyu, the "four quarters," if not a completely centralized state, at least was meant to be such. It would be unjust not to credit the Incas with some sense of economic and social planning. The records can be interpreted in many ways, and the road network is still there as witness of their desire to unify their conquests under one government.

Among all the evidences of high civilization that the wondering Spaniards noted as they penetrated further into the Inca empire, none astonished them more than the quality of the roads. They bestowed eulogies on them in their first reports, enthusing about their width—eight horsemen could ride abreast—the walls which bordered them, the blocks of stone with which they were paved, the streams that ran beside the roadway, and finally the trees which shaded the travelers. The conquistadores would have been yet more enthusiastic had they known, as they found out later, that the coastal road stretched 2,500 miles and led to the heart of Chile. Later they found the road, crossing mountains, valleys, and plains, joining Ecuador to Argentina. Transverse roads from the highlands to the sea completed the network whose total length has been estimated at 9,500 miles.

We have reason to be astonished that so much effort was put into building roads whose sole users were travelers on foot and their unique beasts of burden—the llamas. Was it really necessary to make them so wide and with such a smooth and solid surface? Is there not in all this something gratuitous, or rather vainglorious, which can only be explained by the pride of these despots with armies of workers at their command? These roads, and the megalithic Inca monuments, show us with what prodigality the Cuzco sovereigns spent, even wasted, their main source of wealth, the

115

Suspension bridge

strength, patience, and time of the Andean peasant, the *hatun-runa*.

The Andean rivers, running through steep gorges and subject to violent floods, presented a difficult problem to the Incas. They had no timber at hand with which to build bridges, and since the principle of the arch was unknown to them, they could not dream of using stone. They overcame these obstacles by making suspension bridges, such as were in use in Peru until quite recently. Cables as "thick as a man's thigh" were made of cabuya fiber and stretched from one bank to another, where they were fixed to beams and anchored, for greater security, to stone pylons. A network of finer cords joined the cables, forming the sides and floor. The Spaniards, while admiring the ingenuity of the Indians, confessed that they could not cross these bridges, swayed by every wind and sagging dangerously in the middle, without a shudder of fear. Nevertheless, they managed to get their cavalry across them.

Those living near a bridge were responsible for keeping it in good condition and renewing the different parts at short intervals. That they attended scrupulously to this may be seen from the fact that the bridge over the Apurímac, built in the fifteenth century, was only abandoned in 1890.

Along the roads, at distances of between eight to fifteen miles, the traveler would find a *tambo*, translated by the Spaniards as "inn." It was simply a shed or a group of buildings built around a courtyard or enclosure. The Inca and his officials stayed there, and it was supplied with fuel and provisions by the neighboring communities responsible for its maintenance. The usefulness of such "inns" in desert or mountain country was too obvious to have escaped the Spaniards' notice, and ten years after the conquest they made a list of them all, and took measures for their continued maintenance.

Finally, no doubt as to the efficiency of the Inca administration can survive the descriptions we have of their postal service. Each village along the road had to supply messengers, *chasquis,* chosen for their speed and endurance. They were put into huts a short distance from each other so that the stage could be covered at top speed. In order not to lose a minute, the *chasqui* announced his approach by blowing on a conch shell, at which the runner for the next stage came to meet him, took the message, and set off. News thus spread with the greatest rapidity. It needed no more than five days for the Inca in his palace at Cuzco to get news from Quito, 2,200 miles away. In this way the emperor was informed of revolts breaking out in his territory or of attacks threatening his most distant frontiers.

Let us now contrast the system described above with Bertrand Russell's celebrated definition of socialism:

Socialism means the common ownership of land and capital under a democratic form of government. It implies production carried on for use and not for profit, and the distribution of the product, if not equally to everyone, at least with only such inequalities as are justified by the public interest.

The Inca empire can hardly be described in this way. The people were subject to the despotism of a ruling caste; its aristocratic tendencies were accentuated as a result of the authority bestowed on petty kings and local chiefs by the conquering Incas. Moreover, in addition to the traditional privileges enjoyed by the *curacas* were those accorded to them as the Inca's deputies. An increasing distance, then, separated them from their former subjects. Agrarian collectivism only existed at community level, the level of the *ayllu,* and was in reality an old system, found alike in the Old and New Worlds. It is thus an unwarranted anachronism to apply to a neolithic collective a term only suitable for industrialized societies.

Production was only partially directed to the needs of the people, for all the surplus went to the ruling class and its officials. It is true that part of the surplus was redistributed in the form of food and equipment for workmen and soldiers, or as gifts to nobles, priests, and officials. Help to the old and sick, which one is tempted to compare to our social security legislation, was the task of the village, not the state. This obligation simply expresses the old-fashioned solidarity of the group, still found among the primitive farmers of Amazonia and among the peasants of modern Peru.

Socialism, as experts in this subject have underlined, is not limited to the common ownership of property, but also requires that the property be dedicated to the good of the community. In the Inca empire, the tribute paid as labor service and in manufactured goods benefited only the caste to whom it gave wealth and power.

The classical tradition that the Spanish chroniclers have set up has obsessed the minds of modern historians and sociologists, who have assiduously compared the Inca empire to ancient Rome, modern states, and utopias, but have never thought of likening it to the conditions which prevail, or have prevailed, in societies wrongly called primitive.

For instance, there is more than one similarity between the Inca empire and the old kingdom of Dahomey. This state was founded as a result of successive conquests made by the kings of Abomey. It had an internal organization often quoted as an example of high administrative ability in a people still in an archaic stage of civilization. Like the Incas, the kings of Dahomey recognized the autonomy of agricultural communities and left their traditional chiefs in place. These, in the same way as the Indian caciques, were integrated with a hierarchy of officials, the high ranks of which were recruited from the royal family. The King of Dahomey also had to be kept informed of his kingdom's resources, and had censuses taken of the population, divided into age groups. The payment of taxes and the levying of troops were carried out with the greatest rigor. The state was feared and obeyed. The king's inspectors, the *recaderos,* exercised the same authority as did the *tokoyrikoks,* the Inca's men. The women the villages supplied to the king were formed into a female army, in place of being shut into "convents" to serve the nobles or the gods according to the Inca usage. These analogies are only given as examples. They help to show that a kind of bureaucratic administrative system can well arise in an illiterate people, whether American or African.

The conquistadores were used to fighting "naked savages," and were dazzled by the appearance of an advanced civilization among people they were naturally inclined to regard as unreasoning barbarians. They were particularly struck by the discipline that pervaded the empire. Later, the old order appeared the more humane and just because of the misfortune and cruelty introduced by the Spaniards. Faced with the horrors of the conquest and colonization, the despotism of the Incas was remembered as a golden age. Indeed it was so to the extent that the Cuzco emperors, more perhaps by the force of circumstances than by good judgment, ruled their subjects well, and by imposing the *Pax Incaica* led them to prosperity and happiness.

Religion

The religion of the Incas, as far as our knowledge goes, seems to have been a mixture of nature worship, primitive fetishism, animistic beliefs, theological notions, and subtle, complex ceremonies with a strong leaning toward magic. It was to some degree a reflection of the Inca state itself, where a social and economic structure that had remained in many respects archaic was combined with an enlightened administration, and where very different civilizations were fused in a single melting pot.

The religion's chief ingredient was sun worship. Inti, the Sun, ancestor of the dynasty, became the imperial god. His celestial power was the counterpart of the *Sapa Inca*'s rule on earth; his worship merged with the homage paid to his son. Thus it was from political as much as from pious motives that the Incas raised temples to Inti in all the conquered territories. The deduction has been made that the Incas, like the Catholic kings and the caliphs of Islam, burned with proselytizing zeal and were bent on imposing a superior religion on benighted "barbarians." These are, however, false analogies due to the Spanish chron-

Gold idols

iclers' readiness to interpret Indian behavior in the same light as their own. The Incas, like the Pharaohs, sought to establish the sun cult throughout their empire in order to bestow a religious gloss on their imperialism and to form a bond between themselves and the subject peoples. They were not hostile to local religions, but demanded that in every province a privileged place should be accorded to their ancestor, the Sun.

Of all the Inca gods it was the Sun who was served by the greatest number of priests and "chosen women"—four thousand in Cuzco alone. The widest lands and largest herds belonged to him, and he it was who received the richest offerings of gold and silver and fine cloth. When the emperors returned triumphant from a successful campaign, they would dedicate a part of their booty to him. Pachacuti, after defeating the Collas of Bolivia, "gave many of the things that he had brought back with him to the temple of the Sun God and to the mummies of his ancestors that were kept there." The priests of the Sun were held in higher esteem than those of other gods, and exercised more authority.

The great Temple of the Sun at Cuzco, the fabulous golden precinct of Coricancha, was a building of great magnificence. As Solomon's temple to the Jews, or St. Peter's to the Roman Catholics, so was Coricancha to the Incas. It attracted countless pilgrims and served as a model for many lesser temples in the provinces.

While its size was impressive and the masonry of its walls particularly fine, the architecture itself was primitive. It consisted of a number of rectangular buildings, little more than large thatched sheds, arranged within a vast enclosure, thus following the same plan as the private dwelling of a family group. The temple was situated in the lower town between the rivers Huatanay and Tullumayo, upon a terrace whose supporting walls soared upward to form the dwellings of gods and priests. The outer surfaces of the enclosure walls, almost 1,300 feet in length, and of the shrines within them, were decorated with a frieze about a foot high made of thin gold plates nailed to the masonry. Gold of better quality was used on those parts where sunlight fell than on the parts always in shadow. In the Coricancha there was a little garden where, during the festival of sowing, the Inca would symbolically break the earth, and where, three times a year, imitation maize shoots with stalks, leaves, and cobs made entirely of gold were planted. These artificial plants, mentioned in the inventory of Atahuallpa's ransom, must have started all the fantastic stories about a marvelous golden garden where the trees, grass, birds, insects, and even the life-size figures of the guards and their llamas were all made of pure gold. A number of modern historians have taken these romantic fantasies quite seriously.

The Sun God's pre-eminence in the Inca pantheon is easily explained by dynastic interests. It is more difficult to account for the cult of Viracocha, the Creator, which tended to replace that of the Sun God, who was reduced to a mere creation or "son" of the Supreme Being, from the reign of Pachacuti onward. This change in the hierarchical order of the gods must surely have been wrought by an intelligent clergy given to theological specu-lation and basing their conception of the supernatural world on the earthly one they knew; but the motives of the emperor in carrying out this reformation are less clear. What interest could Pachacuti have had in lessening the prestige of his ancestor, the Sun, in favor of Viracocha, the Creator? When he placed above all the nature gods a god whose dominance was undisputed, since he was the Master of Creation, was he encouraging the cult from inward conviction or from policy? A tradition passed on by the Spanish chroniclers suggests that Pachacuti (others say Huayna Capac) had genuine doubts about the pre-eminence accorded to the Sun. If that benevolent star ripened the crops and fertilized the earth, he could hardly be the ruler of the uni-verse. What was one to think of a god who was forced to work like a day laborer and to appear and disappear in order to make night and day? "What sort of Lord was that? Was he not ob-scured by clouds for weeks, even months, at a time?" There is nothing to prove that any such ideas—ideas that would not have been alien to a Catholic missionary—had ever occurred to Pacha-cuti; nevertheless the emperor's devotion to Viracocha is attested by the sudden importance that the cult of the Supreme Being took on in the official religion.

Viracocha was the special protector of Pachacuti, to whom he had appeared in a dream before the decisive battle against the

Chancas. As a sign of gratitude he built a temple at Cuzco, where the god was represented as a golden statue "the height of a ten-year-old child, standing up, with its right arm raised, the hand almost closed, thumb and index finger held up as in one who commands." Pachacuti also established centers for the worship of Viracocha "in the capitals of various provinces, and saw that attendants, herds, pastures, and estates were devoted to the god's service."

The majestic figure of Viracocha has always fascinated students of the Inca religion. Some have supposed him to be the supreme deity of the mysterious race that built the megalithic monuments of Tiahuanaco, and that the figure carved on the lintel of the Gate of the Sun is his. According to them, the Incas were the heirs of the Tiahuanaco civilization and therefore imposed the religion of their predecessors on their own people. There is no need to postulate any such relationship to explain the origins of the Viracocha cult. Behind the "venerable Lord, the distant Lord, the most excellent Lord" we can distinguish a figure familiar to us in the mythology of every Indian tribe from Alaska to Tierra del Fuego. He is the "Old Man of the Sky," the "Maker of Earth," "The Ancient One"; world creator and culture hero. In the primitive cosmogonies he is often a vague being, a sort of awe-inspiring shadow, whose sole function is to provide an explanation of how the world began. At his side there is usually a second mythological being, the "Transformer," who completes his work and instructs the people in the rudiments of civilization.

Insofar as his character can be discerned among the confusion of ill-reported myths, Viracocha is at once Creator, Culture Hero, and Transformer. He manifests himself in successive acts of creation. First he makes heaven and earth, and a race of men who dwell in darkness. These men, for some unspecified sin, he destroys, changing them into statues of stone. In his second manifestation he emerges from Lake Titicaca and at Tiahuanaco creates "the sun and the day, the moon and the stars." That done, he carves from the rock "men with chiefs to rule over them, women great with child, women who have already given birth, and babies in their cradles," in short, all the peoples of the world, whom he then commands to disperse to the four corners of the earth, where he has provided land for them.

The world thus peopled by all the different nations and tribes known, Viracocha ceased his function of Creator and changed into the Culture Hero. He gave men "laws which they must keep on pain of destruction." For some time he wandered over the Andes in the company of a mysterious fellow traveler in whom we recognize the "Deceiver" of Indian mythology, a stupid, scatterbrained character, whose aim it is to thwart the Culture Hero.

It is said that before he created the world Viracocha had begotten a wicked son called Taguapica, who set himself up against his father in everything. When the former created men virtuous, the latter corrupted them in body and soul. If the father raised up mountains, he made plains, and he turned his father's valleys into hills. He dried up the springs his father had caused to flow and, in short, opposed him in all he did.

After many adventures, that gave rise to various natural phenomena, Viracocha reached the coast, where he cast his mantle on the sea and, using it as a raft, vanished over the horizon. This runs parallel to other myths of the Culture Hero who, after he has fulfilled his mission and showered benefits on mankind, departs toward the setting sun to reside in the country of the dead, often uttering a prophecy that he will eventually return to save the world and bring renewed happiness or, on the contrary, to destroy his work.

Among the Indian tribes the Creator and Teacher is rarely regarded as the chief god. If the Incas did not banish him to a distant heaven, it was because they placed him in a pantheon where there were other gods with well-defined spheres of influence. The cult of Viracocha was the concern of priests and court, so that the collapse of the empire proved fatal to his worship. Within a few years the ordinary Indian, who remained so deeply attached to certain nature spirits and local totems, had forgotten him. It is only through a Spanish priest, Father Cristóbel de Molina, collecting at Cuzco in 1575 some dozen hymns to Viracocha, that we have any authentic knowledge of that god's character. The lofty idea of the Creator held by his priests, and the style of the prayers in the Quechua language addressed to him, have suggested that Christian influence may have been involved. Professor Rowe, however, who has succeeded in restoring the hymns to their original version, is convinced that they owe nothing to the missionaries' teaching. The forms and expressions used are basically different to those of the Christian liturgy in the Inca tongue.

In these prayers Viracocha is described as the creator of the Sun and other gods, of men and of their food. He is compassionate and kind. Where is his dwelling place? No one knows. "Where art thou?" the singer asks. "Without? Within? In the clouds or in the shadow? Hear me, answer me, and grant my prayer."

He is entreated to protect the crops against frost and hail, to cause men to multiply and their resources to prosper. They look to him to watch over the Inca, whom he has created, and to grant him victory over his enemies with rich spoils of war. "May his people and his servants increase and his enemies be confounded. Keep his sons and his children's children in peace for ever and ever, O Lord."

All these prayers reveal a deep longing for peace and security. "Let me live in peace and security. Let thy people live in peace and security. Those whom thou hast made protect and lead by the hand." He is also reminded that, since men are his creations, it is for him to watch over them and their welfare.

The following is a translation of two prayers to Viracocha preserved for us by Cristóbel de Molina.

O Lord, happy and fortunate Lord of victory, who hast pity
upon men and holdest them in affection, ensure that those who serve
thee, the poor and wretched, those whom thou hast created and set
upon earth, may live in peace and safety with their children, their
sons, walking in the path of righteousness; raise not temptations, that
they may live long without interruption or disaster, let them continue to
eat, let them continue to drink.

O faraway and ancient Lord, O most excellent Lord,
Who hast created and established all things,
Saying: Let there be man, let there be woman.
Thou the molder, thou the Creator,
Inasmuch as thou hast made and established mankind,
Grant that I may live peaceably and in safety,
O Lord, O generous and diligent Lord, most excellent Lord,
Multiply thy people,
Increase the number of thy children and multiply them. . . .

The prayers quoted above are among the rare vestiges of Inca liturgy to have survived the shipwreck of that civilization. To those broken fragments can be added one more hymn to Viracocha, miraculously preserved by Yamqui Salcamaygua Pachacuti, a seventeenth-century Indian chronicler. For profundity of thought and soaring lyricism this much-quoted text can bear comparison with the loveliest of the Psalms. Its beauty is unquestionable, in spite of the rather free translations and finishing touches that have been applied to the obscurer passages. The version below is taken from the Spanish translation recently made by J. M. Arguedas, the outstanding Quechua expert. What it has lost in clarity and charm it has gained in authenticity. One has only to compare this translation with the prayers to Viracocha collected by Molina in 1575 to realize that they all belong to the same literary and religious traditions.

To Viracocha, power over all that exists, be it male or female,
Saint, Lord, Creator of newborn light. Why art Thou? Where
art Thou?
Is it not possible for me to see Thee? In the world above, or
in the world below,
Or wheresoever in the world Thy mighty throne is to be found?
In the heavenly ocean or the seas of the earth, where is Thy
habitation? O Pachacamac,
Creator of man,
Lord, Thy servants desire that their feeble eyes may
behold Thee. . . .
The sun, the moon, the day, the night, the summer and the winter
are not free:
From Thee they receive their instructions, and Thee they obey. They
approach that which has already been ordained. . . .
Where and upon whom hast Thou bestowed Thy shining scepter?
With a joyful mouth, with a joyful tongue, day and night shalt
Thou call. Fasting, Thou shalt sing with the voice of the nightingale.
And perhaps in our joy, in our good fortune, from whatever corner of
the world, the Creator of man, the Lord almighty, shall hear
Thee. . . .
Creator of the world on high and of the world below, Creator of
the mighty ocean, Vanquisher of all things, where art Thou? Speak,
come, Truth from on high, Truth from the deep, Molder of the
world, Power over all that exists, sole Creator of man, ten times
will I worship Thee with my feeble eyes.
What splendor!
Before Thee will I prostrate myself. Hear me, O Lord! Give ear unto
me O Lord!

Pan pipes in stone

And you, O rivers and waterfalls, and you, O birds, lend me your
strength and all that you can, help me to cry out with your throats,
with your desires, and remembering all things, let us rejoice and
be happy. And thus, with swelling hearts, let us depart.

We know that these hymns were sung, but no single piece of
authentic Inca music has come down to us. The immediate ban
that fell on the rites of Viracocha and the Sun God, as well as
other traditional rituals, combined with the introduction of
Spanish music during the sixteenth century, changed the native
Indian music profoundly. We hear it now only in very adulter-
ated form, and so-called "Inca" music is really a hybrid of native
and foreign elements.

Fortunately, Inca music has not disappeared without trace. A
fraction of it has been preserved by oral tradition, and the
originality of its structure enables us to pick it out from among
the music composed under European influence. When the songs
of modern Peru are analyzed in this way, they confirm the
evidence of the ancient Peruvian wind instruments as to the
kind of scales then in use. They were always pentatonic. According to M. and Mme. d'Harcourt, the typical features of

Playing the pipes of Pan

Peruvian pentatonality were: (1) the descending curve of the melody; (2) the frequency of the scale *sol-mi-re-do-la,* with the characteristic interval of a minor third (*do-la*) which often comes at the end of the melody; (3) the long disjunct intervals during the course of its development.

We have no evidence of any big vocal choruses and can only suppose that, since these are absent in modern Andean music, polyphony was also unknown to the Incas and that the men and women sang in unison.

After Inti, the Sun God, and Viracocha, the deity most revered by the Incas was Inti Illapa, the Storm God, the ruler of rain and hail, the hurler of thunderbolts. He ran about the heavens armed with a club and sling. The mighty crack of the sling sounded like thunder to mortal ears. The Indians saw his shadow in the sky, outlined by the stars of the Great Bear beside the vast river of the Milky Way, from which he fetched water to pour down upon the earth. One of the religious poems of the Incas preserved for us by Garcilaso, however, gives a different explanation of the rain.

Fair maiden! Now your rain-making brother breaks your little pitcher; and that is why the thunder roars and the lightning flashes and the thunderbolt is loosed. With these pure waters, royal daughter, you send us rain and sometimes hail and snow. He who made the world, the God who gave it life, great Viracocha, bestowed upon you your soul and set you there that you might fulfill this task.

Illapa, in his aspect of rain giver, was especially honored by the peoples of the empire. He had many temples, some of which became famous. When drought threatened the crops the faithful would assemble on the mountaintops to pray and offer him sacrifices. His image or symbol was displayed beside that of the Sun in the great square at Cuzco, and an effigy of him was carried, like the Inca, in a gold-encrusted litter. The Moon was worshipped as wife and sister of the Sun. Her symbol, a silver disk, stood near the image of the Sun.

The primitive tribes of the Amazon attribute to every animal or even vegetable species a "spirit" that watches over their increase and guards them from useless destruction. With the Peruvian Indians this belief developed into the worship of certain groups of stars in which they perceived the likeness of a celestial animal, patron and guardian of its earthly counterparts. Our constellation of the Lyre (Lyra), for instance, looked to them like a llama with its mate and little one. Shepherds would entreat it to cause their flocks to prosper. In the same way they traced the outline of a great cat among the stars in Scorpio, and set up a cult in its honor. The Pleiades were given the title of "Mother" and great festivities greeted their appearance.

The official religion of Cuzco was a thing apart from those popular beliefs we mentioned when considering the anthropomorphized nature spirits represented by idols. The theological preoccupations that the imperial caste and the priesthood expressed in their worship of Viracocha were no concern of the

Ancestral figures, Chachapoyas

peasantry. Nevertheless, the Incas' piety, like that of most of their subjects, extended also to a great many *huacas,* fetishes. These could be natural phenomena such as mountains, hills, lakes and caves, or man-made objects such as temples, chapels, palaces, pillars, and tombs. Many of the *huacas* owed their sacred character to some personal connection with one of the Incas. A house might become a cult object merely because an Inca had built it or visited it or slept there. Thus it was said of the *huaca* Cugitalis that "it was the place where Huayna Capac had dreamed of a certain war. The dream came true, whereupon he decreed that the spot should thenceforth be holy ground." A spring might be declared sacred because an Inca liked to bathe in it: "The spirit of the spring would be beseeched not to take away the Inca's strength or let any harm come to him."

When a royal person had thus conferred a share of his holiness on such a place or object, the sacrifices or offerings dedicated to the *huaca* were often made with the purpose of persuading the invisible spirit to grant health, prosperity, or victory to the Inca. Some *huacas,* however, did not owe their sanctity to any association, real or imaginary, with the reigning dynasty. Ciro-coya, for example, was a grotto believed to be the breeding place of hail, and the Indians would leave offerings there to turn away that perennial scourge from their fields. According to local super-stition there was, near the Temple of the Sun, a place where earthquakes were born. By sacrificing children, llamas, and pre-cious stuffs there the Peruvians tried to ward off those disasters.

It is thought that there were nearly five hundred *huacas* in Cuzco and its immediate neighborhood. These followed imagin-ary lines, called *zekes,* radiating from the Temple of the Sun. They were also equally divided according to the four quarters of the empire and the two districts of the city, the "upper town" and the "lower town." The upkeep of these shrines and the sacrifices offered there were the charge of the family groups of Cuzco, either because the *huaca* lay within the bounds of their property or because its spirit was supposed to be the supernatural guardian of the *ayllu.*

Ethnologists have solemnly debated whether the Indians made a distinction between the spiritual element and the material ob-ject that represented it. The question did not arise. The *huaca,* whatever it was, was a sacred object, and as such, had super-natural powers that it was wise to conciliate. That was all that mattered.

The *huanquis*, those stone statues that had once been the "brothers" of the Incas, and from which they were never long parted, came under the heading of *conopas* or guardian idols: Pachacuti's was a figure of the Thunder God.

A calendar to regulate the sequence of religious feasts and agricultural labors was all the more necessary since the Incas used lunar months in their calculations and had the greatest difficulty in getting them to correspond to the solar year. How they achieved this is not known. To determine the season for sow-ing more or less accurately, one of the emperors, possibly Pacha-cuti, had four little stone towers built along a mountain ridge west of Cuzco that were visible from a platform situated in the center of that city's main square. "The two middle towers were nearer together than the others. When the sun reached the first tower it was time to prepare for sowing and when it set between the two middle ones it was time to sow at Cuzco."

Huaca, Kenko, Cuzco

Some of the chroniclers, Garcilaso de la Vega in particular, held that the Incas could tell the exact date of the solstice and equinoxes, but this claim must be treated with some reserve. Furthermore, the phases of the moon were of only secondary importance to them and it is unlikely that they had a ten-day week.

Religious festivals occupied an important place in Inca life. Every month had its celebrations lasting several days, or even weeks, at a critical period such as the solstices, the gathering in of the harvest, or the paying of tribute. There is insufficient space here to list all the information supplied by Cristóbal de Molina, Coba, and Garcilaso de la Vega on the subject of these festivals.

The glory of the Sun, that Inca of the heavens—and by reflection that of his earthly counterpart—was celebrated in June, at the winter solstice of the southern hemisphere. The *curacas* and the "great lords of the land" were always present at these splendid ceremonies, called *raymis:* they "hastened there to worship their God and show respect to their king."

On the day of the festival the Inca left his palace accompanied by all the members of his family in order of rank and age. Thus they came to the great square of Huacaypata

where they waited, barefoot, for the Sun to rise, their eyes turned to the east. As soon as it appeared they knelt down in adoration and, with their arms spread out before their faces, they threw kisses in the air, saying that the Sun was their father and their God. . . . Then the king rose up alone and took in either hand a great cup filled with his usual beverage and, as eldest son of the Sun, invited the God to drink from the cup in his right hand. They believed that the Sun accepted and bid the Inca and all his family drink with him which, to the Indians, was the highest proof of friendship and goodwill. After the Inca had invited the Sun to drink he poured on the ground the liquid from the cup he held in his right hand. . . .

The great September festival called *sitowa* was certainly the most interesting, both for the religious ideas that inspired it and for its drama. The occasion was dedicated to ritual purification and to the driving out of all the evil spirits that might menace the city. The people assembled in the square and at the rising of the new moon they cried out, "Disease, disaster, misfortune, leave our city!" The cry was taken up all over the town, and by four groups, each of a hundred soldiers, that were stationed on four roads corresponding to the four cardinal points. These warriors, armed from top to toe, then began to run along the roads toward the "four quarters of the empire." Still other groups repeated the exhortations and, spear in hand, chased the invisible evil spirits to a place some five or six leagues outside the town, where they stuck their spears into the ground "to show that the evil spirits were to stay within those bounds and might not cross the line of spears."

Their aim achieved, the runners bathed themselves in the river and dipped their weapons in the water so that the taint of evil should be washed out to the sea. Meanwhile the inhabitants of the town came to their doors and shook out their clothes, crying, "Go away troubles! Happy festival day! Creator of all things, may we live till next year to see another such festival!" After a night spent in singing and dancing they went to bathe in the springs and rivers to wash away the last remnants of evil. Torchbearers "chased the evil spirits of the night with flaming brands, having already killed the evil spirits of the day with spears." In every house a sort of paste called *sanko* was prepared from maize. This the inhabitants smeared on their bodies, on the threshold of the house, and on the larder, as one last measure to expel "diseases and weakness."

The mummies of the Incas, as well as the statues of the high celestial gods, were carried to the great square at Cuzco, where they were "warmed"—that is to say rubbed—with *sanko*. The temples and idols were treated in the same way. At the imperial palace these rites were assigned to the eldest uncle of the emperor.

Pure white llamas with the thickest fleeces were immolated in front of the sacred statues so that their blood fell onto the *sanko* paste and moistened it. This the priest tasted, after pronouncing a curse on anyone who took part in the ceremony with a "divided will or a divided heart," or who would offend against the gods or the emperor. Everyone, including children and invalids, ate some of the paste made holy by the sacrificial blood.

Parallel to the hierarchy of government there existed an ecclesiastical establishment over which the Incas had secured control. A priest's rank depended on the temple he served and the functions he fulfilled there. In the religious hierarchy the primacy belonged to the high priest of the Sun, the *Vilca-oma*, always a near relation of the Inca—his brother or uncle. He led an austere life, subject to many taboos, within the precincts of the Temple of the Sun. His assistant priests formed a sort of clerical college and were all nobles or scions of noble families.

In the provinces the local *curaca* families provided the priests for the Sun Temples and important *huacas*, while each village set apart certain of its inhabitants to serve the cults of the local deities. The following figures will give some idea of the place occupied by the clergy within the empire. More than four thousand persons were employed in the Coricancha in various capacities. This figure included the actual priests, of course, the Virgins of the Sun, all sorts of attendants, the shepherds of the holy flocks, the porters, and the sweepers. It has even been claimed that there were more people in the service of the temples than there were in the army. We know from Pedro Sancho the conquistador, that in the Temple of the Sun on an island in Lake Titicaca "there were six hundred Indian attendants and a thousand women occupied in preparing *chicha* to be poured as libations on the holy rock known as Titicaca."

No Inca institution has aroused more curiosity than the Virgins of the Sun, whose Quechua name, *acllacuna,* simply means "chosen women." They were selected by special officials from among the young girls of each community, and shut away in convents until the moment came for the Inca or his deputy to decide their fate. Those who were not chosen to be the emperor's concubines, to be given to high officials, or to be reserved for human sacrifice, were attached to the temple. There they prepared the ceremonial food and drink, especially *chicha,* which was consumed in huge quantities at the festivals. They also ran workshops, where they produced cloth of the highest quality, the renowned *kumbi,* made from vicuña wool. The garments made by the *acllacuna* were reserved for the emperor and his family, the priests, and the idols, or were offered up as sacrifice. Each *acllacuna* convent was set under the authority of a woman who was considered the bride of the Sun God. The largest and most famous of these establishments was at Cuzco and consisted of more than 1,500 women.

The priests performed many different functions, but did not necessarily specialize exclusively in any one of them. Their names varied according to the part they were undertaking, whether diviner, immolator, confessor, or medicine man.

It could be said that the Incas, like the ancient Romans, were the most superstitious of men. No important action was undertaken without prior recourse to divination. It also had a judiciary value. If it was a question of finding a guilty man, discomforting a recalcitrant prisoner who denied his crime, or a sinner concealing his fault, the auspices were consulted. It was in the practice of this art that the survival of ancient Andean shamanism was most evident. There were special priests whose mission it was to invoke the spirits that they might reveal knowledge of the future or of hidden things. The most spectacular of these occasions were those on which the dead were summoned through the flames of a brazier. To ensure their benevolence the priests would sacrifice white llamas, objects of gold or silver, or even children. The ghostly voices then came up from the flames, which rose and fell by means of a copper-tipped or silver-tipped tube, blown by the priest. The purpose of this fiery conjuration was to unmask traitors. Some of the temples contained famous oracles, such as those of Pachacamac and Lima. When Hernando Pizarro penetrated the Holy of Holies from which issued the voice of the oracle, he found nothing there but a rough-hewn stake encrusted with gold.

For purely private concerns, the soothsayers confined themselves to observing the wanderings of spiders, the arrangement of coca leaves on a plant, or the track of saliva running over their fingers; when the destiny of the nation was at stake they consulted the entrails of animals slaughtered for sacrifice. Sometimes they would inflate the lungs by blowing into the windpipe, and read the future by the layout of the veins. Another method of divination was to count the grains in a head of maize or the pebbles in a heap, and prophesy good or evil fortune according to whether the sum was even or odd.

The ritual of confession, to which the Incas resorted in certain circumstances, was seen by the Spaniards as a hideous parody of their own religious custom. When the Inca form of confession was assimilated into the Catholic Church, its significance was changed. To the Incas "sin" meant violation of ritual or offenses against the social or natural order which provoked divine wrath and called down public disasters. Any acts of sorcery or the least malediction against the holy person of the Inca were crimes that could be expiated only by confession and acts of penitence. If the rains were late in coming, or frost spoiled the crops, or the emperor was ill, it was a sign that confession and expiation were demanded to restore the balance of nature. According to circumstances, the onus of confession to a *hocha,* ritual error, could fall on a single individual or on the whole community. The sinner had to prepare himself by a five-day fast. After this the

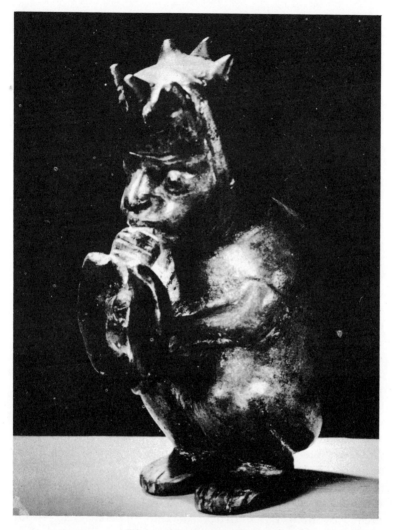

Diviner blowing into lungs

priest heard his confession, bidding him keep nothing back. In any case, had the sinner tried to conceal his guilt, the examination of a sacrificed animal's entrails, or some similar method of divination, would have unmasked him. The confessor then gave the penitent's back a few light blows with a stone and said some prayers, after which they both spat on a handful of herbs and sent it floating down a river. Sometimes the guilty would wash away their sins in water, or submit to various religious restrictions.

The fields and flocks dedicated to the temples provided the greater part of the sacrifices offered to the gods. On the other hand, a private person wishing to conciliate the deity had to depend on his own resources. The nature of the sacrifice exacted was decided by divination.

The llama was the chief sacrificial beast. The number and color of the victims were regulated by complicated rules, the knowledge of which was the first requirement of priestly learning. Llamas for the Sun God had to be white, for Viracocha, brown, and for the God of Thunder, particolored. The beast was led around the statue of the god and then, while facing toward it, its throat was cut. The blood was collected in a bowl containing various kinds of flour and thrown toward the four points of the compass. When the offering was only for a minor deity, or if the suppliant was a poor peasant, a guinea pig was considered good enough.

Apologists of Inca civilization, such as Garcilaso de la Vega, draw a veil over the custom of human sacrifice, which was, in fact, a general practice, either by denying its existence or by soft-pedaling its importance. It is true that the Incas never indulged in the holocausts dear to the Aztecs, but they nevertheless sacrificed human victims to their chief gods and *huacas*. In addition to the regular immolations, men, women, and above all children were sacrificed every time divine mercy seemed to be specially needed: at the beginning of a new reign, if the emperor was gravely ill, if some part of the country was devastated by earthquakes, or some calamity threatened the empire. The children sent from the outlying lands to imperial temples for sacrifice were part of the tribute the provinces were forced to pay. The bodies of the little victims had to be flawless; the least skin blemish would disqualify them. Before they were killed the children were well treated. On the day of sacrifice they were fed, or if they were still babies, their mothers suckled them, so that they should not "enter the presence of the Creator hungry or crying." Most of them were buried alive, but in certain cases

Conopas

their chests were cut open and the heart torn out, as in Aztec Mexico. The still-beating heart was offered to the idol, and the idol's face daubed from ear to ear with its blood. The bodies were buried in a special cemetery near the sanctuary. Some of these burial grounds have been dug up by archaeologists, notably at Pachacamac on the coast.

Among the quota of girls that the provinces provided for the Incas there were always some who, sooner or later, would be sacrificed to the gods. Yearly, when a share of the tribute was doled out to the provincial temples, the chief sanctuaries were granted human victims. These were kept in enclosures near the temple until the feast day came when, decked in jewels and wearing their finest clothes, they would be led to the idol to be strangled or slaughtered. First, however, they were benumbed with *chicha* and told that they were "called upon to serve the gods in a glorious place."

Food offered to the god was cast into a fire lit by embers from a sacred flame that burned eternally within the precinct of the Coricancha, a flame fed with fagots of aromatic wood. Basketfuls of coca leaves were likewise offered up to the gods—an offering above price, for only the Inca and those near to him might consume that herb, reputed to possess mystic virtues.

An enormous quantity of woven material was sacrificed to the *huacas.* As well as *kumbi,* wooden figurines draped in miniature garments were cast into the flames. Little images of gold and silver were burned in the shrines or hung on the sanctuary walls as offerings. Lastly, the people sought to please the gods with gifts of shells, *mullu.*

Libations were made with *chicha,* either by sprinkling it on the ground with the fingers, or pouring it by the cupful at the feet of the god. At Cuzco the emperor emptied goblets of *chicha* into a stone vat covered with plates of gold.

The Inca City

Inca civilization developed at a time when towns were growing up all over the Andean region. The Inca contribution to this urban tradition was one of their surest titles to glory.

The Incas were great builders of towns. They made of Cuzco a real metropolis that each emperor, at least from Pachacuti onward, delighted in embellishing, taking advantage of the resources in manpower and raw materials that his conquest brought him. In the conquered provinces they moved some of the population into the towns they were creating, thus foreshadowing the policy later adopted by the viceroy Toledo at the end of the sixteenth century. Can one really talk of Inca town planning? Although the chroniclers may tell us that the sovereigns had their architects make clay models of the towns or buildings they proposed to construct, this is only a tradition. The regular placing of roads crossing each other at right angles and opening into squares, as in modern Latin America, suggests that the Incas had a rational conception of how a city could be laid out. Excavations of Inca towns, where the ruins can still be seen, impress

Machu Picchu

one with the almost "American" aspect of the general plan: big squares, a checkerboard pattern of streets, and large blocks of buildings enclosed, on the coast at least, with walls. This triumph of the quadrilateral is perhaps not so much a result of conscious planning, as the result of the kind of architecture and shape of Inca cities. Many towns were no more than a collection of *kanchas,* that is, three or four houses placed within a rectangular enclosure. Besides the towns that seem to have been planned, there are others which appear to have grown by chance along roads or paths leading to a center occupied by temples or palaces. Many Indian cities were, above all, a collection of public buildings inhabited by priests and officials. The lower orders of people attached to these dignitaries were lodged in huts which have left no trace. That is why the ruins of some magnificent buildings appear to stand in the middle of places that have never been inhabited. The supplies needed by the people living in these religious or administrative centers came from the neighboring villages. Even Cuzco, described to us as a great capital with a population, doubtless exaggerated, of 300,000 inhabitants, was no more than a collection of villages and market towns spread around the temples and royal residences. After the conquest, the villages became independent parishes, later transformed into districts of the modern town, but still keeping their old names.

The imposing bulk of the Inca ruins and their magnificence tend to overshadow the simplicity of the basic architectural plan. Palaces, temples, and houses all reproduce the humble Quechua peasant's hut (surviving still in the Andean valleys), though on a grandiose scale. Four walls in dry stone or mud, a gabled roof covered with thatch, a door and a few niches inside, are the components of even the most complicated structures. The monotony of the design and the heavy severity of the façade were redeemed by its bonding. No civilization in the world has been able to assemble such enormous blocks of stone with such perfection. This is why isolated or half-destroyed walls can still move us, even though we cannot reconstruct, even in imagination, the building to which they once belonged.

The best examples of Inca masonry are found in Cuzco, though there is little left of the Inca city, burned down by the Indians themselves in their last effort to drive out the invaders. The

Fortress of Kanchari

Spaniards in turn demolished it to build their Spanish city, and it was finally ravaged by several earthquakes, not the least of which was in 1952. Most vestiges of Inca building are now only to be seen in the foundations of colonial period buildings. The walls are constructed of many-sided blocks fitting one against the other like a jigsaw or Chinese puzzle, or alternatively rectangular blocks in regular courses. Not long ago, archaeologists credited the polygonal block bonding of the "cyclopean" type to a megalithic empire dating from a period well before the one that centered around Tiahuanaco. The Incas, heirs to this mysterious civilization, though good architects, were held to have made no attempt to show their skill by building with such huge worked blocks. In fact it has now been proved that both styles, the

146

Fortress of Pukara, Cuzco

polygonal or cyclopean and the regular courses, are contemporary and do not go back beyond the fifteenth or even the sixteenth century. These two styles, though used at the same time, probably derive from two different cultures. Rowe has put forward the theory that the rectangular walls with regular courses and a slightly convex face reproduce, in stone, walls made of turves cut from marshy soil, whose surface is smooth but where each turf is separated from the next by a deep groove. The big polygonal or cyclopean bonding he held to have originated in walls made of huge blocks of irregular stone, which would explain the depth of the jointing. Cellular bonding, made of small polygonal stones, is derived from the former. The most perfect Inca masonry is seen in a third type of bonding, in which rec-

147

tangular stones are cut with such regularity and fitted so carefully that a perfectly smooth surface is achieved.

The different kinds of bonding do not represent different stages of architectural development, but simply the different functions of the walls. Big irregular blocks were used for walls, terraces, and enclosing "courts"; rectangular blocks were preferred for the main part of a building. Both types of masonry were sometimes combined in building a palace or temple—for example rectangular bonding might surround a doorway in a wall of cellular construction.

The stone came from quarries four to fifteen miles away. They were moved on sledges traveling over rollers, and put into place by means of ditches and earth ramps. The blocks were quarried with stone tools and copper or bronze chisels. They were ground down or rubbed against the neighboring stones for a long time until the fit was perfect. It has been noticed that big blocks are often flanked with smaller stones, the latter being those the masons used for grinding against the larger stone, after having inserted a thin layer of wet sand between them.

The principal characteristics of Inca architecture are the trapezoid shape given to doors, windows, and alcoves, and the bosses, or tenons, projecting from the surfaces of buildings. The purpose of these additions has never been clearly accounted for. In some cases they were pegs, to which ropes to secure the thatch could be fastened; in other cases they were just ornaments. Most Inca buildings had only one story, but buildings with an upper story were fairly frequent at Machu Picchu. The temple of Viracocha was exceptional in having three stories.

Modern Cuzco, in spite of the Inca foundations of its buildings and the Indians gliding silently along the alleyways, is an Andalusian town. Even the Inca remains offered for the admiration of tourists often do not date back to pre-Hispanic times, but are buildings put up by Indian masons for their new masters at the end of the sixteenth century. Only the three Spaniards sent by Pizarro to supervise and expedite the collection of Atahuallpa's ransom ever saw the town in its full splendor. The first Europeans to reach it, they got there in 1533, when the temples had not yet lost the gold plates which decorated the walls like a cornice. The town seemed so big that they reported "one could not see it all in a week." They were equally impressed with the roads, "well laid out and paved."

A few months later Pizarro and his army took possession of Cuzco. Here is the description of it given by Pedro Sancho de la Hoz, one of the conquistadores:

The city is the most important of all those in which these Lords dwell and is so beautiful that it is worthy of being seen in Spain. It is full of lordly palaces and there are no poor people in sight. Every nobleman builds his palace there, and so do all the caciques, though they do not live there permanently. The majority of these buildings are in stone and others are half-faced with stone. There are many houses in adobe and they are very well laid out; the streets are in a checkerboard pattern, very narrow, all paved and with water channels running down the middle. Their sole defect is their narrowness, for on each side of the channel there is only room for one horseman. The city is built on the side of a mountain and on the neighboring plain. The main plaza, almost entirely flat, is square and paved. Around it are the houses of four nobles [read "Incas"] who are the rulers of the city. The buildings are painted and of cut stone.

The town was dominated by the enormous fortress of Sacsahua-mán, one of the most surprising buildings in the New World, equaling the pyramids of Egypt in the amount of work put into building it and the impression it produces in the onlooker. Standing in front of its triple rampart of cyclopean masonry, its defense buttresses, salients, and narrow gates with gigantic jambs, one does not know what to admire most; the sheer mass of the blocks—some of which measure more than thirteen feet in height —or their fitting together, which is as perfect as a piece of carpentry work. Sancho de la Hoz saw it before it was ruined and said:

It is the most beautiful thing to be seen in this land. The ramparts are made of such huge stones that no one seeing them could suppose they had been placed there by the hand of man. They are as big as pieces of mountain or rock, and some are thirty hands high and others are just as large, some of twenty-five and others of fifteen hands, but there is not a single one small enough to be transported by even three carts. They are not just loose stones, but well fitted one to the other. . . .

The ramparts were in three terraces which were dominated by three towers, two square and one round. Besides its cisterns the citadel contained a palace and an arsenal full of military stores.

After the Conquest

After the Cajamarca ambush and the capture of Atahuallpa, a strange apathy seems to have overcome the Indians. The army made no counterattack, nor did the Indians rise in mass to rescue the emperor and drive out the intruders. The aggressive inclinations of a few Inca chiefs were easily nipped in the bud or overcome. The Indians accepted the exactions and brutality of the Spanish soldiers with resignation and without apparent anger. When Pizarro left Cajamarca he was followed by long files of Indians reduced to servitude.

Appalling abuses, stupid destruction, and needless atrocities had to be committed by this band of adventurers before the Indians, pushed beyond endurance, abandoned their peaceful attitude. The first revolt against the white men was led by a son of the emperor Huayna Capac; he had the name of the founder of the dynasty—Manco. This man, who saved the honor of the Incas and who hoped to restore the land of Tahuantin-suyu, had started by being a collaborator. Instead of opposing the advance of the Spaniards to Cuzco, he joined with them and, under

comendero
ÕELCOMENDEROLE
haze ahorcar al cacíq̃ prencipal don ju cayanchire y por su
Ale conten to alen̄ com en de ro le tue lg̃ael conreg̃or

Spanish justice

their command, made war against the generals of the faction of his half brother Atahuallpa. The reward for his services was to be "crowned" emperor by Francisco Pizarro, who allowed, or perhaps insisted on, the observance of the old ceremonial. The mummies of the dead emperors were brought out into the big square at Cuzco to welcome their descendant, and the bards intoned the traditional hymns glorifying the deceased Incas.

From 1533 to 1536 Manco was less than a puppet Inca; even the nobles of his own court did not trouble to pay him the respect due to an Inca. When his brother rebuked them for their disgraceful behavior, he was publicly slapped in the face by Francisco Pizarro. In spite of himself, the unfortunate Inca was dragged into the quarrels between Almagro and Pizarro. Once, threatened with death by the Pizarro faction, he had to hide under Almagro's bed. Held responsible for isolated Indian attacks on the Spaniards, he was imprisoned, at first in his palace and later at Sacsahuamán. The scoundrels who guarded him raped his wives in front of his eyes. As if that were not enough, they amused themselves by using his nose as a candle snuffer and by urinating over his body, the body of a living god. Manco had once fought Quizquiz, his brother Atahuallpa's powerful general, in a spirit of revenge and had thus helped defeat the remaining opposition to the invaders, but these last humiliations were too much for him and filled his heart with an implacable hatred of the Spaniards. This made him the first great leader of the Indian resistance movement. Under the pretext of delivering a big golden statue to his jailer, Hernando Pizarro, Manco managed to escape and reach the Yucay valley. From there, at the head of a big army, he launched an attack on Cuzco. So numerous were the Indians answering his call that "by day they covered the plain like a black cloth and by night their fires were like the stars of the sky." (Pedro Pizarro)

To destroy the Spaniards, who had dug themselves in, the Indians did not hesitate to burn their own capital. They set the thatch alight by firing red-hot sling stones, or flaming arrows, and attacked by jumping from wall to wall, thus avoiding the cavalry. They managed to force their adversaries into the central square, much in the way that beaters drive game. Although in a desperate situation, the Spaniards managed to take the fortress of

Sacsahuamán, a place held by 1,500 Indians. It was at this moment of disaster that an Indian chief called Cahuide, a man who had fought bravely, chose to throw himself from the ramparts rather than be captured.

With an army estimated at 40,000–50,000 men Manco could not defeat 200 Spaniards. The desperate courage and superior armament of the latter is not enough to explain Manco's defeat. Manco might well have had the advantage of numbers, but he did not have his father's seasoned troops. His army consisted of peasants who, though infuriated by the Spaniards' depredations, lost heart when faced with a long siege. When the time of sowing came around, they deserted in mass to go and till the fields for the next crop. Manco changed the traditional Inca tactics. Well knowing that the Spanish cavalry "was the best fortress to oppose the Indians' fury," he sought to overcome that danger. He provided his men with *bolas* to throw at the horses' feet and bring them down, or he lured the cavalry on toward country strewn with pitfalls. The Indians had captured a few horses and Manco, mounted on one of them, charged the Spaniards lance in hand. The Indians also tried to use the arquebuses they had captured, but since they did not know how much powder to load, these arms were more dangerous to themselves than to the enemy.

Though the Indians realized they had to use new methods of warfare, they did not give up, unfortunately, their old customs and taboos observed in time of war; consequently, as custom demanded, they chose the full moon to attack, so losing the advantage of surprise and allowing the Castilians to use their cavalry.

The big uprising which Manco had counted on to swamp and overcome the invaders having failed, he modified his plans of attack and decided to wage a war of attrition from a number of strong points. He first established himself at Ollantaytambo, but having been driven out of that town, he went deeper into the Andes and took refuge at Vitcos, no doubt an old military post and one which was to become the center of Inca resistance for forty years. The exact situation of this town was a mystery for a long time. It was known to be in the Vilcabamba Andes, and very inaccessible; even today the region can only be reached by climbing mountains more than 16,000 feet in height, crossing raging torrents in deep ravines, and following steep paths often hidden by thick forest. The Spaniards long hesitated to risk their lives in country so well protected naturally, where a handful of men could guard the approaches even against numerous and hardened troops. Vitcos, the Incas' last capital, was visited by very few Spaniards. One of them, in an account of his journey, reports that "there was a large expanse of flat ground covered with sumptuous buildings skillfully and artistically constructed in stone."

Up to quite recently, the region Manco made his kingdom presented so many obstacles to travelers and colonists that it was a complete *terra incognita,* in spite of its proximity to Cuzco. The American senator Hiram Bingham swore he would find the fabulous capital of the last Incas, and in 1908 explored the length and breadth of the Vilcabamba Andes, looking at even the smallest archaeological remains. After a long search and some perilous climbs, the Indians took him to Rosaspata, in the Urubamba valley, to some ruins which seemed at all points to correspond with the scanty information available about Vitcos. He was impressed, as were those rare visitors to the spot in the sixteenth century, by the trapezoid door jambs and lintels, made of granite as white as marble. Any lingering doubts he might have had as to the identification of the site were dispelled when his guides showed him, near the old town, an enormous white granite rock above a spring. A flight of steps and some cylindrical objects carved on it showed the rock to be a *huaca.* It could be no other than the famous "white rock," mentioned in the Calancha account, near to which was a Temple of the Sun the Spanish missionaries had had the audacity to burn down; in fact, near the rock some ruins of a building, which must have been a sanctuary, were still to be seen.

Some iron objects which Bingham picked up in the ruins of Rosaspata bore witness to its postconquest occupation and were further evidence of the site being that of Vitcos. It must also be remembered that it was in searching for Vilcabamba that Bingham climbed the crest on which the ruins of Machu Picchu lay hidden in the forest; it became the most celebrated dead city of the continent.

In his Andean retreat, Manco Capac reestablished the Inca

way of life as far as he could. He was followed into his voluntary exile by many nobles, who were said "to have torn themselves with regret from the pleasures of Cuzco and elsewhere." The Inca also took with him "great treasures and many changes of clothing in fine wool." In addition he managed to save from the conquerors' greed the statue of the Sun God and the mummies of some of his ancestors. Worship of the great gods of the empire was restored. Priests and "chosen women" were attached to the service of the gods and the old court etiquette was imposed on the nobles. We should not look on the zeal shown by Manco Capac in resurrecting the old imperial pomp, even in a reduced form, as the obstinacy of a prince filled with the old traditional ideas of Inca glory and blind to any innovation. In fact, the founder of the new Inca state was well endowed with the warlike virtues and political capability of his ancestors. He was a true statesman—the last his dynasty produced. He understood that, to face the Spaniards with any chance of success, he had to adapt himself to the strangers' methods, those methods which had led to the defeat of his race. We saw above that Manco Capac had formed a troop of cavalry and had given arquebuses to his soldiers. Articles of European origin were no doubt sold to the Inca rebels by Spanish traders, who took coca, tobacco, and cocoa in exchange. Manco Capac, consciously or not, did his best to combine the old and new civilizations. Isolated though they were, in one of the most remote and inaccessible regions of the Andes, Manco Capac's subjects were more influenced by their enemies than many Indians in daily contact with the colonizing Spaniards.

The situation of the Incas, cut off in their mountains behind precipices and forests, reminds one of the position of the Spaniards themselves after the battle of Guadalete, in Asturias, when they formed their last line of defense against the invading Arabs. The analogy, no doubt, was not lost on the Spaniards. The desperate eagerness they put into the destruction of this little Inca state may well have been based on the fear that it might become, in its turn, the starting point of a "reconquest."

From his capital, Manco never ceased harrying the Spaniards in every direction. He managed so successfully to cut their lines of communication that Pizarro was obliged to found the town of Huamanga (Ayacucho) to keep the road open between Lima and Cuzco. Secretly he incited the Indians to rebel, and a number of revolts that broke out in upper Peru were encouraged by him. He punished collaborators severely and even tried to starve out the Spanish by destroying the crops of his own subjects. For seven years he made it impossible for any settlement to become permanently established in the south of Peru. However, he did nothing on the coast.

Manco carefully followed the quarrels that divided the conquistadores. During the civil war between the followers of Pizarro and the supporters of Almagro he had hoped that the bandits would all succeed in cutting each other's throats, and that he would remain master of the field. But such was his hatred of Pizarro and all his family that he supported the young Almagro, who had assassinated Francisco Pizarro to avenge his father. Young Almagro was fleeing toward Vitcos after his defeat, when he was captured. Diego Mendez and a few more of his followers managed to take refuge with Manco, who welcomed them with open arms. These men, whose lives the Inca had saved, repaid his kindness by assassinating him, perhaps with the idea of buying their way back into the viceroy's favor. However, Manco's bodyguard killed them before they could get away on the horses stolen from their benefactor. Manco's body was embalmed and put in the Temple of the Sun beside those of his ancestors.

Manco Capac was succeeded by his son Sayri Tupac, a ten-year-old boy. This seemed a propitious moment for the Spaniards to secure the submission of these people without having to resort to a costly expedition, the outcome of which could be most uncertain. They used the numerous relatives of the young Inca to carry out the negotiations, relatives who had stayed in Cuzco and who could bear witness, by their luxurious mode of life and the privileges they enjoyed, to the advantages of collaboration with the conqueror. The proposals made to Sayri were tempting: his person to be respected, two palaces at Cuzco, the revenues from a rich estate, and the title of *adelantado*. When he was of an age to make his will felt, Sayri decided to accept the proposition against the advice of his councilors. This capitulation was put out as a freely taken decision and one agreed to by the Sun and the Earth Mother, whom the priests had consulted. In 1555, Sayri

BVENGOBIERNO
LAPRECIÕDETOPAA

maco ynga   ynfante Rey lo lleua preso conguco
rona el capié   tan martin   garcia meoyo la-

oyoča

Tupac Amaru enters Cuzco

Tupac, his forehead bound with the imperial *llautu,* his luxurious litter escorted by three hundred warriors, took the road to Cuzco, where the viceroy received him with honor. He died in 1560, in the Yucay valley, of poison, it is said. His daughter, Doña Beatrix, married a nephew of Saint Ignacio de Loyola, and his granddaughter was the Marquesa de Oropesa.

After the death of Sayri Tupac another of Manco's sons, Titu Cusi, high priest of the Sun, had himself proclaimed Inca. The legitimate heir, his younger brother Tupac Amaru, was shut up in a convent of the Virgins of the Sun "as was the custom of this country's sovereigns before the coming of the Spaniards."

Titu Cusi, who gave the Inca state its last flicker of life, had good reason to hate the Spaniards. As a child he had been their prisoner, and it was only with difficulty that he escaped sharing the fate of his father when he was assassinated in front of his son's eyes. He resumed hostilities, but more in the style of a robber chief than of a sovereign. His warriors were content to pillage the farms in the settled territories. From these raids they returned with booty and prisoners, who increased the meager Inca forces.

Titu Cusi's opposition to the Spaniards was less bitter than that of his father. All the time he was fighting them he never stopped negotiating for the concessions granted to his brother Sayri. Had he given up all hope of winning and was he trying to get the best terms possible for becoming a well-provided-for collaborator, or was he trying to gain time by useless preliminary discussions? We do not know. In the course of the struggle, which went on for ten years, a few Spaniards were allowed to enter the Inca's territory. One of them was Diego Rodríguez de Figueroa, who has left an interesting and detailed account of his curious mission to the military camp that was the dissident Inca's court.

Scarcely had Rodríguez de Figueroa crossed to the left bank of the Urubamba when he was surrounded by a group of be-feathered, menacing Indians wearing "masks," who told him that unless he was a man of courage he had better return home and not appear in front of the Inca, who could not abide cowards. Several days later, after a hard journey over the steep and well-wooded mountains, the envoy from the royal audience was led into the presence of the Inca, who had come to Bambacona to receive him. A kind of theater with a floor of red earth had been prepared there. Titu Cusi had his face "masked," and wore a headdress of various colored feathers and a silver breastplate. He had feathered garters from which wooden bells (*sic*) were suspended. He carried a shield and a golden halberd in his hand and was armed with a golden dagger in the Spanish style. He was surrounded by bodyguards, also wearing feather headdresses, and silver and gold ornaments encrusted with jewels; they were armed with halberds. The nobles crowding around the Inca first addressed the Sun and then their sovereign, to whom they said, "Son of the Sun, you are the son of the day . . ."

Titu Cusi made no mystery of his feelings toward the Spaniards. After a drinking party at which the soldiers had performed a war dance, the Inca seized a shield and spear and, addressing Rodríguez de Figueroa, cried, "Leave at once, and bring me all the men from behind the mountains. I want to fight the Spaniards, kill them, and throw their bodies to the wild Indians to be eaten." He then paraded before the Spaniard some six or seven hundred Indians armed with bows and arrows. "He shook his lance once more and said he could raise all the Indians in Peru, and that if he gave the order they would fly to arms." The noble *orejones* threatened Figueroa with their weapons, shouting, "Death to the bearded ones."

In spite of these threats Titu Cusi's role was somewhat ambiguous. He let his guest know he was not hostile to the Roman Catholic religion and recalled that he had been baptized. He denied ever having given orders to burn down chapels, of which act he had been accused. In the end he agreed to meet a Spanish official to discuss the terms of his capitulation, though after having agreed and being asked to implement his promises, he fell back into defiance and evaded all meetings.

Toward the end of his reign Titu gave some evidence of his desire for peace. He was baptized under the name of Philip and allowed two Augustine monks to preach in his state. The monks took advantage of the good will and patience of the Inca. They never stopped their reprimands and set fire to a sanctuary of the Sun God. The Inca limited himself to expelling one of the troublemakers and kept the other, Father Diego Ortiz, close to him.

The Inca suddenly fell ill, and the Indians, believing in the power that the missionary said he had from God, asked him to save their ruler. Father Diego Ortiz was unwise enough to accept the challenge and even to give medicine to the Inca. It proved as ineffective as his prayers. Deceived and in despair, the Indians threw themselves on the missionary, whom they tortured to death.

The funeral of Titu Cusi was celebrated with the traditional rites. The imperial insignia—the red fringe, the mace, the parasol, and the golden ornaments—were paraded with great ceremony for the last time. Then the young Tupac Amaru, who was still shut in a convent of the Virgins of the Sun, was sent for.

Tupac Amaru's reign was extremely brief. The unrelenting viceroy, Francisco de Toledo, had decided to destroy this shadow of an Inca kingdom, which he pretended to believe was no more than a resort of rebels and brigands. He had a pretext to hand in the assassination of one of his emissaries and in the death of Father Diego Ortiz, who was set up as a martyr to the faith. The inhabitants of Cuzco were called upon to provide a contingent of men who, helped by Cañari auxiliaries, left to conquer the Vilcabamba region. For some mysterious reason (Calancha assures us that the Inca territory had been devastated by an epidemic and by famine), the Indians not only failed to guard the defiles, but also failed to cut the suspension bridge over the river Urubamba giving access to their territory. Consequently, the Spaniards had no difficulty in getting hold of Vitcos and of breaking the weak resistance offered them. The Inca, tracked down on all sides, was captured before he could take refuge with the Amazonian forest Indians.

If Tupac Amaru thought the Spaniards would respect the royal blood of which he was issue, or the title which had been bestowed on him, he was greatly deceived. The chains that weighed him down only made more derisory the royal insignia with which he was surrounded when he entered the capital of his ancestors, barefooted, in the middle of the prisoners and loot that the white conquerors dragged behind them. The trial of the Inca was conducted as iniquitously as was that of his great-uncle Atahuallpa. The Indian "captains" were the first to be executed. They had been so cruelly tortured that most of them died before reaching the scaffold. Here is an eyewitness account of the last moments of the last Inca to wear the *maskapaicha*:

He was led through the streets of Cuzco between Father Alonso de Baranza, a Jesuit, and Father Molina, preacher to the Indians. They instructed him and offered him consolation for the benefit of his soul. The scaffold was placed in the middle of Cuzco's main square, in front of the cathedral. The Inca was followed by four hundred Indians, enemies of his ancestors, marching lance in hand.

All the covered spaces, as well as the roofs and windows in the parishes of Carmenca and San Cristóbal, were so full of people that an orange thrown among them would not have reached the ground, so tightly were they packed together. When the executioner, a Cañari Indian, unsheathed the cutlass to be used for the execution, a strange thing happened. The crowd of Indians gave such a cry of grief one would have thought that judgment day itself had come. Even the Spanish spectators showed their sorrow with tears and sad faces. When the Inca saw this he raised his right hand in a noble gesture and let it fall. He alone was calm. All this noise was followed by a silence so profound that there cannot have been a living soul among all the people in the square, or near it, who moved. The Inca spoke with an eloquence unusual in a man about to die. He said his life had run its course and he deserved his fate. He implored all those who had children never to curse them for any bad behavior, but only to punish them; for once, as a child, he had annoyed his mother. She had cursed him and prophesied he would die by execution and not from natural causes. And now that was coming true. Fathers Carrera and Fernandez contradicted him and explained that his fate came from the will of God, and not from a mother's curse. Of this they were able to convince him, for they had the eloquence of Saint Paul. The Inca repented of his words. He asked everyone to forgive him and told the viceroy and magistrate that he would pray to God for them. The Bishop of Popoyán, Don Augustín de la Coruña, and some other priests hastened to the viceroy to implore him to spare the Inca's life. They urged he be sent to Spain to be tried by the king himself. Nothing would move Don Francisco de Toledo. He sent Juan de Soto, a law officer of the court and a servant of the viceroy, on horseback wielding a staff to clear his passage. He galloped up furiously, his horse crushing many people. He gave the order to cut off the Inca's head at once. The Inca, having received the last rites from the priests, put his head on the block like a lamb. The executioner came forward; taking the hair in his left hand, he cut off the head with a single stroke and raised it for the crowd to see. The moment the head was struck off all the cathedral bells were rung and the bells of all the monasteries and churches in the town. The execution caused the greatest sorrow and brought tears to everyone's eyes. The head was impaled on the point of a lance, near the scaffold. It became more beautiful every day, for the Inca had been a handsome man. At night the Indians would come to adore the head, until one morning, at dawn, Juan de Sierra by chance went to his window and

BVENGOBiERNO

ATOPA·AMARO·L·ECOR

TAN·LA·CAVESE·ELCV3CO

ynca uana caui may tam un qui sapra au cachiccho mana hui yayocta

conrayquita   cuchon

Execution of Tupac Amaru

saw this idolatrous worship indulged in by the people. The viceroy was informed. He had the head buried with the body in one of the cathedral chapels. A pontifical mass was sung for the repose of the Inca's soul and all the clergy of the town took part in the funeral. Numerous masses, with organ music, were said in his honor, for he had been a great lord and an Inca.

The Spanish conquest of the Inca empire, and the colonial rule that ensued, entailed for the Indians the destruction of their goods, the loss of their most sacred traditions, their utterly ruthless exploitation, slavery, and very often torture and massacre. It is the fashion in Spain to jeer at the "black legend" invented by the heretics to calumniate the noble Iberians. But the detractors of Spanish colonialism are less severe in their condemnation than many of the Castilians themselves who witnessed so much horror and oppression. It is no use saying that it is only the followers of Bartolomé de Las Casas who are concerned. The denunciations made by rough soldiers, and by lawyers, of the atrocities and abuses they saw are to the honor of Spain. Even though the Crown tried to protect the Indians' rights, one cannot absolve a regime because the intentions, and only the intentions, of its leaders were often just and generous. It was, of course, difficult for the king and his representatives to get themselves obeyed on the other side of the ocean. "The law should be respected but not obeyed," was the attitude of the Spaniards whenever they were enjoined to stop their excesses. Moreover, those who praise the colonial past, in spite of the historical evidence, too often forget that the abuses and violence, whose echoes resound from the depths of time, are still being practiced in many regions by descendants of the conquerors and colonists. Perhaps if Antonio Ulloa and Jorge Juan were to tour the Andean provinces today, they would hardly need to alter many events recorded in their famous *Noticias secretas de América,* in which they courageously and honestly denounced the treatment inflicted on the Peruvian Indians in the eighteenth century.

One of the first results of the conquest was a brusque fall in population, which went on until 1796, the eve of the Wars of Independence. According to official Spanish statistics, the number of Indians under the jurisdiction of the courts of Lima and Charcas, which is roughly equivalent to modern Peru and Bolivia,

CO REGI MI ENTO

COREG.º² AFRENTAAL

al cal se hor senario por sos gubos que no le da mi tayo.

"The law must be respected"

fell from 1,490,137 in 1561 to 608,894 in 1796; the population had fallen by more than half.

It is presumed that the empire's population fell by 50 percent in the thirty years following the conquest. Those historians who put it at six million estimate the loss at three quarters of the total. Infectious diseases introduced by the Spaniards, such as smallpox, have been held responsible for this terrible mortality, and in fact, diseases which cause little harm to Europeans can easily decimate those not immunized by long exposure to them. Many Amazonian tribes have almost disappeared as the result of an ordinary epidemic of influenza or measles. However, no epidemic is recorded in the period preceding the first census. We are reduced, therefore, to attributing the depopulation of Peru to the causes mentioned above. Besides these, many Indians were massacred when Manco Capac made his last attack on the invaders. The civil wars among the Spaniards were equally fatal for the Indians: famines, resulting from the upsetting of their economic and social life, were added to the horrors of war and colonization.

Later, according to the Spaniards themselves, the Potosí silver mines and the Huancavelica mercury mines were great destroyers of men. Forced labor in the mines contributed directly to Peruvian depopulation, for numerous Indians failed to survive the misery and overwork there, and indirectly, too, for service in the mines filled them with terror; thousands of Indians fled from the provinces that recruited forced labor for the mines to take refuge in those that were exempt. Between 1628 and 1754, the Chucuito province, which had to supply a large contingent of miners, lost two thirds of its population.

The Spaniards' hold over the Indians was secured by the system of *encomiendas*; this was a system by which a Spaniard who had distinguished himself in the king's service was given the care and protection of a number of Indian villages, from which he had the right to exact tribute or labor service. To prevent the owners of *encomiendas* (known as *encomenderos*) abusing their positions, the king appointed certain officials, the *corregidores*, to supervise the administration of the *encomiendas*. The *corregidores*, far from safeguarding the interests of the Indians, soon became their worst oppressors. Part of the tribute also fell to the

The Indians work for the benefit of the church

priests entrusted with indoctrinating the Indians.

The conquest destroyed the social and economic structure of the Inca empire; even the distribution of the population was changed. The viceroy Francisco de Toledo forcibly regrouped the Indians into villages and towns where they could more readily be supervised and more easily assimilated into the new colony. Thousands of Indians had to leave their houses and sanctuaries to live in these new and artificial settlements. All links holding the community together were lost. The titular and ancestral deities were forgotten, titles to property abolished, and the old authorities deprived of their powers. Whole *ayllus* disappeared, or were joined together to form new groups. Innumerable peasants, wrenched from their lands and communities, made up a floating population, some working as servants or craftsmen in the towns and others taking posts with the new landed proprietors, whose serfs they rapidly became.

The *mita* was the labor service owed to the Inca by his subjects. The Spaniards soon saw the advantage of this and turned it to their own profit. They laid claim to the service once given by the Indians to their old monarchs, but the new masters gave them no return as the old had done. Under the Inca regime, the *mitayos*, that is, those liable for labor service, were supported from the state storehouses and were not kept too long away from their villages. The Spaniards used Indian labor to the full and gave nothing in return.

The most terrible *mita* was conscription to the mines, and to the Indians this symbolized the full horror of foreign domination. A seventh of the population of Peru between Cuzco and Tarija worked in relays in the Potosí mines, at an altitude of 15,000 feet, and in the mercury mines too: theoretically the working day was only twelve hours and the miner was free to work for himself on Sundays and during the rest weeks that were, in principle, allowed to him. The fate of the *mitayo* would have been just supportable had the laws established for his protection been observed. They were not only ignored, but were even turned against those they were supposed to benefit. Thus, not only were the Indians not paid the sums due to them, but money was extorted from them in the form of forced gifts and taxes.

The miners' calvary started with the journey, sometimes two

or three months long, from their village to the mine. They left accompanied by their wives and children, many of whom died on the way. When their turn came to go up to the mine, they had to stay there five days and five nights at a stretch; they were formed into gangs or teams of three men each, two sleeping or eating while the third mined or transported ore. Piecework was worse. Each man had to produce twenty-five sacks of ore, each weighing more than 100 pounds, in twelve hours. To get it they had to crawl through narrow galleries and climb unsafe ladders. Not being able to fill these quotas the Indians hired laborers, whom they paid from their own meager salaries which were reduced if the quota demanded was not achieved. They also had to pay for their own candles. The majority of Indians were consequently hopelessly in debt and became slaves in everything but name, inescapably tied to the mine. Potosí was like a ravenous monster gulping down the Indian population. The Indians tried to avoid the *mita* by flight; they took refuge in provinces where this form of tribute was not known and established themselves as laborers on a hacienda. There, though they had lost land and liberty, they were at least alive. Land left by the fugitives was either sold by the community or confiscated by the Crown. This is how some of the big haciendas of modern Peru were first established.

The local authorities, for their part, did their best to supply the contingent needed. When the time came for the conscripts to leave for the mines, chained Indians with iron collars around their necks were to be seen everywhere. Women and children accompanied the miserable lines of exiles, with cries and moans, pulling out their hair and "singing in their own language songs of death and sad laments." The unfortunate travelers took leave of their friends, for they had no hope of returning. Those who could sold all their goods to buy themselves out. Many had no hesitation in "hiring out" their wives and children "for sixty or fifty pesos in the sole hope of freeing themselves from the mine."

The local chiefs were beaten and tortured if they failed to supply the labor demanded. Once an Indian returned from the mines to find his wife dead and his children abandoned. His chief forced him into a gang leaving for the hell of Potosí. The *curaca* answered the wretched man's pleading, saying, "If I do not complete my quota with you, the Spanish will burn me, whip me, and drink my blood." Desperate, the man hanged his two children, "so that they may never serve in the mines," and then cut his own throat with a knife.

To the horror of the mine must be added the horror of the *obrajes*, that is, the workshops making cloth and refining clay. As factories they were not badly equipped for the age, but the working conditions were so terrible that the places were like jails to which Indians guilty of some offense were sentenced. Many Indians preferred to be sent to the mines or galleys rather than work at the *obrajes*. The proprietors of these places recruited child labor so as not to have to pay full wages. These unfortunates, forced to work extra hours, were badly fed and terrorized by the gang bosses.

The relay postal service, which had been so useful to the imperial administration, became another abuse. The villages along the road were forced to feed and lodge any traveling Spaniards, in exchange for which they received nothing but outrage. If they could not supply the pack animals demanded, they themselves had to take the place of these creatures and carry any burdens it pleased the Spaniards to load them with.

Military and spiritual conquest were indissolubly mixed. The treaty Francisco Pizarro signed with the Crown before leaving to discover Peru mentions the conversion of the natives. To begin with, the Indians offered very little resistance to the new religion imposed upon them. Many of the leading families appeared to embrace Catholicism with enthusiasm, as they were aware they would never receive the support of the Spaniards, nor retain their privileges, unless they renounced their "diabolical errors." For the bulk of the Indians, the mass, the adoration of the cross, and other rites were just another official religion, which they accepted as calmly as they had once accepted the cult of the Sun. For some forty years, the Roman Catholic clergy thought they had really succeeded. Their surprise was great when they found, in the first half of the seventeenth century, that, under a light veneer of Christianity, the Indians were as pagan as ever. As the Inquisition had no jurisdiction over them, the Church handed the task of extirpating idolatry to the "visitors," that is, ecclesiastical judges, flanked with notaries and assistants, who journeyed around the villages making the strictest inquiries into superstitious practices and inviting the peasants to confess, and to denounce the idolaters. If the need arose, the suspects were tortured. The degree of repentance determined the severity of the punishment: hardened pagans were whipped or exiled, the relapsers went to the galleys; thousands of idols were destroyed and their sanctuaries pulled down; the *huaca*'s goods were sold by auction and their lands given to a Roman Catholic church or chapel.

The Spanish priests did their best to suppress the native dances, in which they saw "lust," or "lewdness" and "idolatry." Huamán Poma de Ayala's unusual chronicle in which, both by drawings and words, he rebukes the Spaniards for their oppression, entreats the authorities not to destroy the traditional music of the country and not to "frighten and mortify the poor people who, when their work is finished, amuse themselves by having a fiesta during which they sing, dance, and feast among themselves, in the midst of their poverty, without offending anyone." Such a humble request was quite justified. The synodal *Constituciones* of the diocese of Lima insisted on the "suppression of dances, songs, or ancient *taquis* (dances), and the burning of all musical instruments."

These formidable "visits" continued until the eighteenth century. The campaigns had but little success, for the majority of the Peruvian and Bolivian Indians are still semipagan today. The "visitors," too, realized the uselessness of their efforts, and did not hide their confusion in the face of the passive but obstinate opposition of the Indians.

The priests were often as hard and as avaricious as the *corregidores*. During the colonial period the clergy showed strong racial prejudice that was a constant source of bitterness to the Indians and half-castes. It was only with repugnance that they allowed the Indians to receive the Eucharist, and in spite of the express wish of Rome and the King of Spain, they refused to ordain Indian priests, or even a man with Indian blood in his veins. In the *Doctrinas*, the priests refused to give the slightest religious instruction to their flocks even while using police methods to get them to the services. Their sins were expiated by whippings on an exact tariff scale: three hundred strokes for

MALA CONFICION
E P

que yaze los padres y uras dlas doteinas aporrea alas ynas
prenadas yalas biejos ya ynos yalas oras solteras no las quiereo
fezar deedad de beyteanos nose confiesa niay remedio dellas—

A dreadful confession

OTABA CALLE
PVCLLACOCVAMRA

singing and dancing in the old style, fifty for a case of concubinage, twenty-four for missing confession or mass. To these bodily chastisements were added various humiliations, such as having the head shaved.

However, the Indians' balance sheet was not entirely on the debit side under the colonial regime. Their resources were increased by the adoption of new plants and animals brought by the Spaniards. They took them up, first of all, for the purpose of paying their quota of tribute; they then gradually introduced them into the native economy. If they were slow to adopt some plants, such as turnips and broad beans, it is because these merely duplicated a native vegetable already in use. As great lovers of *chicha*, maize beer, they had only a faint interest in the vine. Finally, we must not forget that the different climates of Peru determine what kinds of plants can be grown. European domestic animals were much more readily accepted, for the Indians, being good stockmen, quickly saw the advantages they would get from horses, donkeys, cattle, and sheep; these animals were greatly superior to their own llamas and alpacas. New crafts were introduced at which the Indians soon excelled. In Peru from the seventeenth century onward there were workshops where Indians made furniture, glass, European-style cloth, and silver jewelry. The use of money became general, except in the case of direct trade between Indians, where the barter system has lasted to this day.

Renaissance and Decline
of the Incas

To Spanish eyes the viceroyalty of Peru carried on the old Tahuantin-suyu, the empire of the four quarters, under a new God and a new sovereign. The old provinces, *huamanis*, retained their boundaries. The territories included under the name "Peru" were those within the frontiers of the old Inca empire. It needed the occupation of Spain by a French dynasty, with more abstract ideas of administration, for any attempt to be made against the integrity of the Incas' heritage. In 1717, Ecuador was detached from the viceroyalty of Peru to be added to Colombia.

The Spanish Crown recognized the positions and titles of the Inca chiefs, in whom they saw noblemen comparable to the *hidalgos* of the mother country. The Crown confirmed their rank, and gave great privileges to all who could prove their royal descent or their relationship to a *curaca*. As late as the eighteenth century nobles could still defend their right to a disputed title in the courts. It was socially so advantageous to have a little Inca blood in one's veins that many Creole families falsified their

"Inca blood must be avenged"

genealogies in order to connect their families with the old kings.

Provincial chiefs continued to administer the territories the jurisdiction of which had been given them by an Inca. Many became hard oppressors of their people. Though themselves exempt from tribute, they still levied the tax on their subjects, already bowed down under the demands of the *encomenderos.*

If among the Incas there were rebels and resistance workers, such as the Inca Manco and Titu Cusi, there were still more collaborators. The most infamous of them was Paullu Inca, who remained the Spaniards' friend, in spite of the slap he had received from Pizarro. His servility was rewarded with the *encomiendas* and the palace of Colcampata, the ruins of which can still be seen above Cuzco. While the Inca and his men lived as outlaws at Vilcabamba, his brothers and cousins in the capital were falling in with the new regime and aping the Spanish nobility. Reading the eulogies attributed to them one could suppose that they had no other ambition in life than to dress in the Castilian fashion and ride around on fine horses.

The Jesuits founded colleges for the children of the Indian aristocracy. They tried to turn them into young *hidalgos* with a smattering of Latin and able to write elegant, even affected, Spanish. This new elite, of Indian blood but Castilian education, was naturally Roman Catholic and quite unaware of the common people's "superstitions."

By the end of the sixteenth century and the start of the seventeenth, the Inca nobility was almost entirely assimilated and identified itself with the conquerors. It was a section of the ruling class and to some extent enjoyed its privileges. Consequently it is with some surprise that we find, in the second half of the seventeenth century, a change in the attitude of the nobles toward the lower orders. The humiliation and suffering of the native masses, which had once left the nobles unmoved, became a matter of concern to them. Aristocratic Indians dared to protest against the injustice meted out to their subjects and even planned certain acts of revolt. These pangs of conscience were accompanied by a renewed interest in the history of their race, which ever increased in glory as the memory of it faded. Simple details often bear witness to this return to the native tradition. For instance, Indian ladies had themselves painted in the costume of an Inca princess, and lacquered wooden beakers, the *querus*, were decorated with the old designs, or with scenes borrowed from Inca tradition.

This is the period when a celebrated Quechua play was written, *Ollantay*, considered the most important literary work in that tongue. The first version we have of it dates from the middle of the eighteenth century, and even if it is only a copy of an older text, it must have been written in the seventeenth century by some priest speaking Quechua and fascinated by the Castilian theater.

The theme is taken from a historic episode in the reign of Inca Yupanqui, in the fifteenth century. In the first scene General Ollantay opens his heart to his servant Piqui Chaqui (Flea Foot), about his love for Cusi Coyllur (Star of Joy), daughter of the Inca. Piqui Chaqui, in the midst of his buffoonery, tries to talk his master out of it. On the advice of the high priest, Ollantay confides in the Inca himself, who reminds him of his rank and the inexorable law which forbids a commoner to mix his blood with that of any of the Sun's children. Disappointed and threatened with arrest, Ollantay takes refuge among his own people in the Urubamba valley and rebels against the emperor. Pachacuti discovers that his daughter has been seduced by Ollantay and has given birth to a daughter; he shuts her in a cellar and says she must become one of the "Virgins of the Sun."

The Inca's army, under the command of Rumiñawi, is sent against Ollantay and defeated. In the interval Pachacuti dies and the defeated general seeks revenge. Having scarred his face, he approaches Ollantay's fortress as a refugee. Ollantay magnanimously allows him to take refuge, but the traitor takes advantage of a big festival held at his suggestion to introduce his soldiers into the camp. He captures Ollantay, who is led, a prisoner, in front of the new Inca, Topa Yupanqui, who feels no enmity toward the captive. He pardons the general and gives him Cusi Coyllur and her baby daughter, for the Inca wants sadness to give way to joy.

The plot should convince the least critical reader that it is nothing but a Spanish tragedy with an Inca theme and in an Inca tongue. The development of the action, the protagonists, their ideas, everything in this play bears the stamp of seventeenth-century Spanish drama. Rhyme and meter are also typical of Spanish

178

poetry. Nevertheless, the piece does contain a few incidents from folklore introduced as local color. The Ollantay tragedy, a mediocre play whatever writers blinded by their enthusiasm for the Incas may say, is not the only Quechua play that survives. In the seventeenth century, Spanish priests wrote edifying comedies and tragedies, in the native language, based on the *autos sacramentales* of their own country.

It was just at the time when this nationalism, still sentimental and based on folklore, was coming to life, that the first native rebellions broke out in Peru. Some were simply expressions of anger caused by the exactions of the *corregidores*; others were well-planned and long-prepared revolts. The *curacas*, who might have been considered traitors and collaborators by the people, were often the instigators and leaders of these rebellions.

Some of the rebels were moderates who demanded only modest reforms: the right to proceed against the colonial authorities, access to the ecclesiastical orders and positions, education of the Indians, abolition of labor service, and suppression of forced purchase of useless objects. Others, bolder and more fanatical, dreamed vaguely of the restoration of the Inca empire and complete separation from metropolitan Spain. The earliest sign we have of general discontent, and of a united front between nobles and people, is a memorandum written by a descendant of the Chimu kings, Vincente Mora Chimu, who, allowed to go to Spain, gave tongue there to the complaints and grievances of his people.

The first serious revolt broke out in 1737, and spread over seventeen provinces. It was severely repressed. The next year a conspiracy was discovered at Oruro. A half-caste, who said he was descended from the Incas, led it with the object of restoring the empire. Toward the middle of the century, a certain Santos, a pupil of the Jesuits, telling his followers that he had traveled in Europe and Africa, managed to raise the Campas and Amueshas tribes, among whom the Franciscans had established flourishing missions. The Indians who rebelled at the call of this mysterious person had never been under Inca control, and lived outside the Tahuantin-suyu frontier. Nonetheless, Santos proclaimed himself Inca and, linking his name with that of Atahuallpa, took the title of Apu Inca. Not a single expedition succeeded in capturing this rebel; he melted back in the forest every time he was threatened.

The excitement that Santos Atahuallpa's rebellion caused in Peru led the caciques to consider their responsibilities. It must have been then that the idea of a rebellion to restore the empire took shape. A Franciscan monk, descended on his mother's side from the emperor Topa Yupanqui, preached moderation, and suggested that he should lay the case of the oppressed Indians before the Spanish Crown. He wrote a memorandum entitled "The True Remonstrance and Humble and Grievous Complaint made by the Indian People to Your Majesty." It was printed at Lima, and carrying a number of copies, he managed to avoid the Spanish authorities and board a ship at Buenos Aires bound for Spain. There, with remarkable audacity, he succeeded in throwing a copy of his petition into the royal carriage. The king and the Council of the Indies read it and were favorably impressed, but their good intentions floundered in the quicksands of bureaucracy.

The only revolt that seriously alarmed the Spaniards was that launched in 1780–1781 by a *curaca*, José Gabriel Condorcanqui, better known under the name Tupac Amaru II, which he took in memory of the Inca beheaded in 1572, whose daughter had married one of his great-grandfathers. José Gabriel, who claimed the title of Marquis of Oropesa, was a typical representative of the most privileged class of Indian. Relatively rich, he had been well educated and got on well with the colonial authorities. No personal motive seems to have inspired him to lead the most formidable peasant revolt the Spaniards had had to face since that of Manco Capac. Pity and horror alone seem to have led him to it. For a long time José Gabriel had been interested in the fate of his Indians and had tried to get the abuses from which they suffered stopped. Did he come to the conclusion that his protests would achieve nothing and, exasperated by the excesses of the *corregidores*, give way to a fit of blind rage? The fact is that he gave the signal for the rebellion by hanging a particularly hated Spanish *corregidor*. Sixty thousand Indian peasants followed him, but Tupac Amaru knew little of strategy or politics. He did not know how to use his superiority in numbers, or realize the advantage that surprise had given him in the first victories. He was finally beaten by better equipped Spanish troops; he was captured and condemned to be tortured and then quartered in the main square at Cuzco.

Too much hatred had grown in the Indians' hearts for the agony of Tupac Amaru and his followers to stop the revolt he had started. The Aymara Indians from the Titicaca area, famous in the time of the Incas for their warlike qualities, continued the fight. Their chief, Julian Apasa, laid siege to La Paz, the present capital of Bolivia. This Aymara, no doubt of humble origin, was a remarkable man. He was tenacious, intelligent, and a clever tactician. He tried to make the peasants fighting for him into a real army, practiced in the use of musket and cannon. He organized his quarters like a Spanish town. But he lacked the time to carry through his great plan and failed, as did his successor, Andrés Tupac Amaru. This last revolutionary tried to destroy La Paz, which is built in a valley, by damming the river and then suddenly releasing its waters.

In less than two years, José Gabriel Tupac Amaru had become, in the popular imagination, a fabulous being enveloped by messianic dreams. An Indian, who claimed to be his cousin, raised the province of Huarochiri by announcing that José Gabriel, martyred in the big square at Cuzco, had risen from the dead and, miraculously carried to the kingdom of Eldorado in the depths of the Amazonian forest, had become its king. This insurrection too came to nothing.

The Spanish authorities rightly saw these numerous revolts as a reawakening of the old Inca nationalism, and took a number of steps that clearly revealed the nature of their fears. The genealogies, true or not, of the descendants of the "pagan kings," were submitted to the King of Spain for approval; the rank and function of cacique was abolished; the wearing of old-style clothes and of the imperial fringe—the *maskapaicha*—was forbidden. The portraits of Incas, which "abounded in the houses of the Indians who considered themselves noble, with the object of proving their descent," were confiscated; the conch shells "whose strange, sad sounds proclaim mourning and the bitter memory of the past" were banished. It was forbidden to use the dark clothing that the Indians "wore in some provinces, in mourning for their deceased kings and the conquest, which they judged to have been fatal for them and happy for us." The title of Inca might no longer be added to a signature, because it "had an extraordinary influence on people of that class." Finally, the priests were encouraged to teach the Indians Spanish, with the object of effacing all differences between them and the Spaniards. All the descendants of the Incas were traced and many of them were executed. A group of ninety, including women and children, was sent to Spain, where most of them died in prison.

In 1815, nine years before the battle of Ayacucho at which Peru gained her independence, the Indian caciques launched a new rebellion. Once again it was premature; the Indians were beaten and massacred to such an extent that, when the fate of the Andean republics was being decided, the Indian masses could not make themselves heard, for they had lost all their hereditary leaders.

Some leaders of the "independence from Spain" movement dreamed, somewhat vaguely it must be admitted, of a restoration of the empire of the Sun. In 1801, Miranda suggested giving power to two Incas, one of whom would live in the capital while the other would travel around the country. These two sovereigns would have nominated censors, aediles, and two questors.

At the congress of Tucumán, in 1816, General Belgrano proposed the setting up of a constitutional monarchy with the Incas as sovereigns, for according to him it was only just to "restore this royal house so basely deprived of its throne." They hoped by this to avoid a bloody revolution, for the restoration of the empire would have been received with enthusiasm. Bolívar himself advised the adoption of a monarchical regime for South America and suggested that, in order to remove the odium attached to the title of "king," it should be replaced by that of "Inca," "to which the Indians were so deeply attached." After the victory of Junín, a Peruvian newspaper wrote, "The blood of the Incas will be avenged," and the Peruvian national anthem recalls "the hatred and vengeance inherited from their Inca and lord."

In fact, all these plans were nothing more than romantic and sentimental dreams. The Creole aristocracy was quick to seize power and defend its privileges. It fully intended to free itself from what it called "the Spanish yoke," but it was totally opposed to any change in the state of the Indian masses. Born in the country, the large landed proprietors despised the natives far more deeply than did the metropolitan Spaniards and, moreover, better understood the dangers that could arise from Indian revolts. The colonial regime had exploited and humiliated the Indians, but had guaranteed possession of the communal lands. In spite of the three great principles inspiring the new Andean countries, liberty, equality, and fraternity, the lot of the Indians, far from improving, got worse throughout the nineteenth century.

Bolívar's decree "on the distribution of common lands" (April 8, 1824) is an example of a law which, in fact, achieved the complete opposite of what was in the legislator's mind. Bolívar wanted to establish a native peasantry, and to divide up the common lands so as to make each Indian a small farmer owning his own land. But, at one blow, the local native communities not only lost their court officials and their very legal existence, but the peasants lost all protection against the arbitrary behavior of the whites. Such was the origin of that terrible curse for the Indian—*gamonalismo*—the grabbing of Indian lands by means of fraud. Peasants, divided among themselves and ignorant of the law, were powerless to defend their goods against the machinations of the white men, particularly when these were assisted by local authorities and the judges. It became a game to make some poor, illiterate peasant "sign" papers by which he renounced his rights, or to confiscate his land on some futile pretext. If, in desperation, the Indians rebelled, the national army was always ready to repress them and indulge in a little pillage and rape. The leaders, if not "shot while trying to escape," were beaten to death. Many of the big Andean haciendas, whose proprietors live such pleasant lives in Paris, were built up in this way. The Indians, deprived of their land, became *colonos* or *huasipungos* on the big estates. Politicians and liberal writers often refer to this system as "feudal." They are wrong, since the hacienda really corresponds, in the twentieth century, to the large Gallo-Roman or Merovingian estate, with its tenants and its slaves.

By a tacitly accepted agreement, the *colono* is tied to his master and must give his own and his family's work in exchange for a hut on the hacienda land and the right to till a small piece of ground and to graze some animals. The details of the agreements vary from region to region, but they generally envisage four days of work a week for the owner, not counting many other demands for supplementary duties. The *colono*, moreover, has to be a servant in his master's house for varying periods. It is this right to *pongueaje* that was, and is, where it still persists, most bitterly

Lawyers oppress the Indians

resented by the Indians. In Bolivia, until the 1952 revolution put an end to these abuses, the *pongo* could never come before his master with empty hands, but had to bring him fuel. He was not fed during his service, and, as mentioned in the complaint prepared by the Sacabamba Indians, he had to provide his own food "while the master's dogs, which did not even guard the house but were kept purely for show," were crammed with food before his eyes.

The task of transporting hacienda produce to town fell to the Indians, who had either to supply beasts of burden or to carry the goods on their own backs. When the estates started to use motor trucks, the porterage service was replaced by a monetary tax.

Indian masses

Among the Indians' "grievances" was that regarding "commissions." An unfortunate *pongo* might be sent to fetch a mere nothing—a packet of cigarettes—from the town, even if it meant crossing a mountain range in a storm. The Indian's most dreaded "commission" was one that obliged him to go to the semitropical valleys. These mountain dwellers quite rightly feared the valleys, where their only reward would be to catch some tropical disease.

To the above must be added the "charges," the numerous taxes levied in the form of "presents" to the owner, the tithes and fees paid to the priests, and the state tax (abolished in Bolivia in 1882). In the face of these heavy expenses the Indians' pay was derisory. Even in the modern era the legal minimum was turned to his disadvantage. A proprietor could rent out so many of his *colonos'* workdays to another owner or company and, by charging the new employer the full legal rate, make a handsome profit for himself. The colonial *mita* has thus survived in the land of the Incas, in this detestable form, to this very day. Until quite recently even the Indian's saliva was not his own: when *chicha* is made saliva is needed to help the fermentation, and gangs of Indians were set to chewing maize for this purpose.

This exploitation, pitiless though it was, in no way protected the Indian. If his fields looked good, the *hacendero* would turn him out and take them over; if his flock prospered, he would be forced to sell it at a ridiculous price.

This, briefly, is an account of some of the methods of oppression that have turned the descendants of the Incas into the distrustful beings, shut in and despairingly humble, that we find in the Andean countries. Their spirit may have been broken but not their energy.

The Incas in
the Twentieth Century

What now remains of the civilization we have sought to evoke in this book? Has it become extinct, leaving no trace other than the ruins of its cities, its tombs, and the old Spanish texts describing it? Have its institutions and its beliefs disappeared forever, or do they continue to shape the life of the men who are its heirs?

Six or seven million Indians still speak the language of the lands the Cuzco sovereigns once ruled; it is the *runa-simi*, better known as Quechua. This language is probably more widely spoken today than it was in the time of the Incas. With the exception of Aymara, used by a million Bolivian and Peruvian Indians, and of Uro, used by only one or two hundred people, the innumerable languages and dialects at one time spoken in the empire are extinct. It is due to the Roman Catholic Church that Quechua, which the Incas forced on the conquered races, triumphed over its rivals and became the *lingua franca* of the highlands, from Ecuador to the north of Argentina. It is even spoken by peoples

Indians in the city

never subject to the Incas. Quechua, far from losing ground, gains it every day in the Amazon basin, as it is the language used by the missionaries to convert the savage tribes there.

The Indians feel no pride in their language. To them it seems almost like a prison enclosing them on all sides and from which they want to escape, so as to be better able to look after their own interests and become integrated with the rest of the nation. Often the zeal of the education authorities, who try to teach children to read and write in the language of their ancestors, is imperfectly understood by the parents, who insist that Spanish be taught in the rural schools, and see the interest the authorities take in Quechua as a subtle form of discrimination against the Indians. It is to be hoped that the enthusiasm of left-wing intellectuals and Indianists for all that is Indian, in particular Andean folklore, will lead to a change in this attitude and that the use of *runa-simi*, "the language of men," will again become a subject for pride.

Those Andean Indians who have not yet been reduced to the status of serfs on the haciendas are still grouped into "communities" which, in many respects, derive from the old Inca *ayllus*, though the similarities between the modern *comunidad* and the old *ayllu* are far from clear. The most important of the features common to both systems is the collective holding of certain lands, and the inalienability of others. The plots which each family holds with a clear title can in no case be ceded to a "stranger," that is, a white man, a half-caste, or an Indian not belonging to the *comunidad*. The need to present a united front against the encroachment of the big landed proprietors in the past, and today against the whites and half-castes of the towns and cities, has helped cement the feeling of solidarity in the *comunidades* and has united their members. Thanks to this unity, maintained against all comers, they have survived in spite of all sorts of measures taken to destroy them. These *comunidades indígenas* received no legal recognition until after the promulgation of the 1919 constitution. Today there are even artificial *comunidades*, created with the sole object of appearing as such in the register and thus benefiting from the protection of the state. As in the old days, some of them are divided into two sectors, *hanan* and *hurin* (upper and lower), and their members feel it as a bond between them, or sometimes as one uniting them against the other half.

Struggles and suffering make these Indian villages into little inward-looking communities. Their characteristic way of life is not only the result of isolation and poverty, but also of a sort of deliberate ignorance, described by sociologists as "defensive." By refusing to take advantage of alternative ways of life in the outside world, and in remaining fanatically attached to local traditions and customs, the Indians, insofar as they can, try to keep their social system and values intact. Poverty, long suffered and idealized, has become a virtue. Simplicity in dress and house, and frugality, are for them moral imperatives, though they stand in the way of change and improvement in their standard of life. When the balance between production and consumption is destroyed, by population increase, loss of arable land, or for any other reason, the community does not react by seeking new resources or by increasing crop yields, but by restricting its demands. Every time outgoings exceed production capacity, the community reacts by lowering consumption. It is by reducing the fulfillment of their needs that these groups try to safeguard their integrity.

The basic problem for all Andean Indians is that of land. While at one time an *ayllu* might be deprived of part of its land for the benefit of the Inca or the gods without real harm, today there are few *comunidades* that have a sufficiently large area to supply even the subsistence needs of their growing population, let alone the surplus indispensable in a system coming to depend more and more on the market. "Land hunger" sometimes becomes an obsession. It gives rise to interminable lawsuits between Indians, the sole beneficiaries of which are the *tinterillos*, the shady lawyers who, from the sixteenth century onwards, have lived by exploiting the natives. Knowing he has nothing to hope for from the authorities or the Church, the Indian does not hesitate to rebel when injustice and oppression become too cruel. He is well aware that revolt is hopeless and will be bloodily repressed. The frequency of such uprisings gives us the measure of the Indians' despair.

Indian lands, already insufficient to support a sound economy, rarely belong to a single tenant. The considerable growth of population together with the modern inheritance laws have led to the fragmentation, or rather the pulverization, of landed property.

On the eastern shore of Lake Titicaca there are few properties that have not been divided into fifteen or twenty plots. Many Indians complain of having strips scattered through an area at great distances from each other. Chacuito is a village which appears prosperous and enjoys a temperate climate, but only fifteen or twenty families are able to live entirely from their lands. The rest of the population must earn their living in ways other than by agriculture. Many farmers need more land for stock raising, but such development is not possible because of the shortage of pasture. Indians who increase their flocks are obliged to put some of the beasts on hacienda lands, paying big fees either in kind or labor service. All this has resulted in a flight to the towns which increases every day. In the last century, Lima prided itself on being a "white" city, or at least one of mixed blood; today it has about half a million pure-blooded Indians from the sierras, crowded into shacks in the slums.

In spite of the former unrelenting persecution of idols and idolatry, the modern Indians, while appearing to be Roman Catholics, nonetheless offer prayers and sacrifices to the old Andean deities. The worship of the Sun is not entirely forgotten. God and Christ are sometimes identified with the Sun, and still greeted with the title "Young Lord of the Sun." The Sun gives both strength and health, although he can become ill and can infect water too, by means of the rainbow. The pagan deity to receive most homage in Bolivia and south Peru is Pacha-mama, the "Earth Mother," protectress of crops and animals. A generous and benevolent mother, she becomes assimilated with the Virgin Mary. The scrupulously observed religious rites connected with agriculture are placed under her protection.

There is no chapel, however humble, that does not have its statue of Santiago (Saint James), the warrior saint, protector of the conquistadores, who, looking like a seventeenth-century knight, flourishes his sword and tramples the devil beneath his horse's hooves. But the descendants of the Incas see Santiago as the Lord of Lightning, Apu Illapu. Llamas are sacrificed to him at spots that have been struck by lightning. People born when lightning rends the sky, or who have been struck by lightning and have survived, are credited with mysterious powers, making them magicians and sorcerers. In fact, one cannot practice magic unless

Santiago (Saint James), Lord of Lightning

one has received the baptism of celestial fire.

Besides the great gods derived from pre-Columbian mythology, the Indians worship innumerable spirits, *auki, apu, mallcu,* who live in mountains, rivers, ponds, and lakes. These are the old *huacas* we have spoken of so often before. Whole villages are placed under the protection of spirits symbolized by stones hidden in caves or buried in the ground. Family huts are protected by a spirit, in the form of a cat or a falcon, to whom blood libations are offered.

In the markets, both in towns and villages, there are sections devoted to the sale of the traditional offerings to Pacha-mama and the spirits. Tufts of wool, and silver or gold paper, now replace

Pagan symbols glorify the Christian God

the gold and silver the gods once eagerly demanded. Even so, the most sought-after articles are the fetuses of llamas, sheep, or pigs, for they are a substitute for the sacrificial animal itself and are much cheaper. The Indians have grown poor, and have managed to convince themselves that the gods will now willingly accept imitations of the offerings they can no longer afford.

The numerous festivals of the Roman Catholic Church are the pretext for a rich and varied religious life. To make the Christian festivals coincide with those of the Inca calendar, the Indians have been obliged to give minor Christian occasions a considerable importance. Corpus Christi takes the place of the *Inti-raymi,* the great festival of the Sun. The finding of the True Cross, the third of May, takes the place of the old agricultural rites associated with the harvest, giving rise to dances and rejoicing quite alien to the Christian tradition. The empty months between sowing and harvest are today, as in the past, a time of great gaiety, marked by dances and masquerades. Among the three or four hundred dances recorded, it is not always easy to distinguish those dating from the pre-Columbian period from those which were devised during the colonial period and have thus come under Spanish influence. War dances and craft dances had already been noted by the Spanish chroniclers, but the satirical, miming dances are of more recent origin, as are certain mime dances inspired by the old Castilian theater.

In the Andean countries much is made of the "conservatism" of the Indian. He is blamed for economic stagnation and slow progress. Such hasty judgments are most unjust. First of all, we forget that the ancestors of these same Indians created one of the most original civilizations the world has known, and made an area habitable which was barely so by nature. In addition, we do not sufficiently consider the brutal, if not ferocious, treatment meted out to the sons of the Incas until quite recently, not to speak of the present day, which might have broken weaker spirits. Who could replace the Indians if, as some people wish, they were eliminated? In Bolivia, where a social revolution has made the Quechua and Aymara Indians into farmers owning their own land, land which for centuries they had worked for others, their attitude has changed rapidly. They strip off their feigned humility and adopt a more dignified tone and bearing, dropping the name of Indian and calling themselves *campesinos*, peasants. Indian troops have defended the new regime, and when instructed, the Indians have learned to take a preponderant place in the political life of the country, where they constitute more than half the population. In Peru and Ecuador, where the Indians' standard of life continues to be low, there are signs of big changes in the air. The Indian is no longer isolated. He now moves to the towns, learns Spanish, and enters political life. He is beginning to feel his strength, and accepts less readily the pitiless exploitation to which he is still subjected. The Indian's attachment to his community, and his desire for progress within this framework, can be considered his legacy from the Incaic tradition. Already many

of these native groups, tired of waiting for outside help, have taken their destiny in hand and have modernized themselves. *Comunidades* have built schools, created scholarships for gifted children, and established model farms. A *comunidad* at Mantaro has even built an electric generating station from which it secures a good income. Such collective efforts would not be possible without the continuation among the Indians of the feeling of solidarity and the habit of working together which characterized the old imperial *ayllus*. A still more important fact is that all the Indians speak Quechua and thus feel they belong to a nation, that of the Incas, and that they can oppose the whites and half-castes in the name of their common inheritance. In fact, the highland

Indians, from Ecuador to Argentina, now have a place in a much more uniform culture than they had at the time of the Inca empire. The spread of education has made them familiar with the names of the great Inca emperors, and has taught them about the greatness and happiness of the people once under their rule. When, tomorrow, the Indian masses rise to demand that justice be done and that the lands stolen from them be returned, we shall see a third rebirth of the Incas. This new era will come about when the Indian has been completely integrated into the life of the present states, successors of the Tahuantin-suyu. Revolutions now nearing boiling point in the Andes, by giving back to the Indians their human dignity, will set free immense reserves of energy hitherto wasted.

Not long ago anthropologists in the remote villages of the Andes uncovered a myth, certainly an ancient one, which clearly expresses the nostalgia for the past and the hope for better things in the future. Once upon a time a mythical being called Inca-ri founded the city of Cuzco, where a gold rod embedded itself in the earth. A long time ago he was killed by a white chieftain and the dead man's head was buried near Lima. Since then the head has slowly been growing and one day it will return, complete with its body. This will be the judgment day. . . . The Inca empire will be restored and happiness will once more reign over the ancient land of Peru.

Chronology & Bibliography

Chronology

Evidence of hunters and food gatherers, contemporary with extinct animals, in extreme south of Patagonia. Traces of archaic civilizations discovered in Peru.	About 8000 B.C.
Coast of Peru occupied by settled groups of fishermen, practicing a rudimentary agriculture but not yet making pottery. (Asia, Paracas, Huaca Prieta, etc.)	About 3000
Appearance of pottery among coastal peoples. Great technical progress.	About 1200
Introduction of maize confirmed.	About 800
Chavin civilization flourishing, including Cupisnique, Chavin, and Paracas.	From 700 B.C. to A.D. 100
Intermediate period, known as "Experimenter" cultures, of Chicama, Gallinazo, Salinar, Chanapata, Chirapa, etc.	About A.D. 100 or 200
The "Classical" period: Mochica civilization in the north of Peru, Nazca in the south.	From 300 to 800

So-called "Expansionist" period, during which various forms of Tiahuanaco civilization develop: Huari, Pachacamac, and "Epigonal."	From 900 to 1200
Beginnings of Inca civilization and state, as well as the kingdom of the Chimus, successors of the Mochicas.	About 1200
Reigns of the semilegendary Incas: Manco Capac, Sinchi Roca, Lloque Yupanqui, Mayta Capac, Tupac Yupanqui, Inca Roca, Yahuar Huacac, Viracocha Inca.	From 1200 to 1438
Reign of Pachacuti Inca Yupanqui.	1438–1471
Reign of Topa Inca Yupanqui.	1471–1493
Discovery of America by Christopher Columbus.	1492
Reign of Huayna Capac.	1493–1527
Vasco Nuñez de Balboa discovers the Pacific.	1513
Andagoya makes the first voyage of discovery to the south of Panama.	1522
Francisco Pizarro, Diego de Almagro, and Hernando de Luque agree to set out to discover Peru.	1526
Pizarro lands at Tumbez and discovers the Inca empire.	1527
Civil war between the Inca Huáscar and his half brother Atahuallpa.	1528–1532
Pizarro's third expedition: occupies Tumbez.	1531–1532
Pizarro founds the first Spanish town in Peru, San Miguel (today Piura).	June
Ambush at Cajamarca and capture of the Inca Atahuallpa.	November 16
Assassination of Huáscar on Atahuallpa's orders.	1533
Execution of Atahuallpa after paying his ransom.	August 29
The Spaniards enter Cuzco.	November 15
Revolt of Manco Capac II and siege of Cuzco.	1536
Manco Capac takes refuge in the mountains of Vilcabamba and there founds a new Inca state.	1537
Manco Capac assassinated by the Spaniards.	1545

Reign of his son, who submits in 1555.   1545–1560

Reign of Titu Cusi at Vilcabamba.   1560–1571

The Spaniards conquer Vilcabamba, capture the Inca   1572
Tupac Amaru, and execute him.

The orders of the viceroy Francisco de Toledo take   1572
effect, giving Peru a new political and social
structure.

First edition of the *Royal Commentaries,* by Garcilaso   1610
de la Vega.

Revolt of Santos Atahuallpa.   1742

Revolt of José Gabriel, Tupac Amaru II.   1780–1781

Siege of La Paz by Julian Apasa.   1781

Second siege of La Paz by Andrés Tupac Amaru.   1781

New revolt by Indians.   1815

At the Congress of Tucumán, General Belgrano   1816
recommends the restoration of the Inca empire.

General San Martín suppresses Indian tribute, and   1821
grants them Peruvian citizenship.

Bolívar suppresses communal property, thus threaten-   1824
ing the existence of the native communities.

Battle of Ayacucho, which ensures the independence   1824
of Peru.

Payment of Indian tribute reimposed: *Contribuciones   1826
de indígenas.*

Indian tribute abolished in Peru by President   1854
Castilla.

General Melgarejo seizes the communal land of the   1867
Indians on behalf of the *hacendados.*

Indian tribute abolished in Bolivia.   1881

Constitution of Peru accords legal status to the   1919
Indian communal lands.

Democratic revolution in Bolivia.   1952

Victor Paz Estenssoro, President of Bolivia, carries out   1953
agrarian reforms, of which the Indians are the
principal beneficiaries.

Bibliography

Books about the history and civilization of the Incas have been appearing at intervals for nearly four centuries. With the development of ethnology and archaeology, their number has increased. The most important part of this abundant literature is represented by the Spanish chronicles of the sixteenth and seventeenth centuries. Unfortunately, with few exceptions, these texts, published in limited editions, are not accessible to the general public. Even the English translations published by the Hakluyt Society in the nineteenth century have become collectors' pieces. For the reader interested in the Inca civilization, no modern monograph can take the place of the *Royal Commentaries*, by Garcilaso de la Vega. This has been translated into English by Clements R. Markham for the Hakluyt Society (Nos. 42 & 45); and also under the title *The Incas: the Royal Commentaries of the Inca, Garcilaso de la Vega, 1539–1616,* edited by Alain Gheerbrandt, and translated from the abridged French version by María Jolas. While it is true that this chronicle, written at the beginning of the seventeenth century by the son of a conquistador and an Inca princess to the glory of his mother's ancestors, is no longer accepted as uncritically as in the past, it remains nevertheless unequaled both for the charm of the style and for its wealth of information. Among the accounts of Peru by firsthand witnesses of the conquest, Markham also translated and edited for the

Hakluyt Society *Reports on the Discovery of Peru,* by Francisco de Xeres, in which he included *The Narrative of the Journey . . . from the City of Caxalmanca, etc.* by Miguel de Estete; while Pedro Pizarro's *Relation of the Discovery and Conquest of the Kingdom of Peru* and Pedro Sancho de la Hoz's *An Account of the Conquest of Peru* were both translated and edited by P. A. Means for the Cortéz Society of New York in 1920 and 1917 respectively. A manuscript in which scenes from Inca life are honestly and naively described by the Indian Felipe Huamán Poma de Ayala was discovered at the beginning of the century and published in facsimile by the Paris Institute of Ethnology: *Neuva Crónica y Buen Gobierno* (Codex Péruvien illustré, Paris, 1936).

Studies in French on the Incas are rare. Among the best is *Socialist Empire: The Incas of Peru,* by Louis Baudin (New York, Van Nostrand, 1961). This study of Inca institutions does not respond much to the requirements of modern ethnology. *Daily Life in Peru at the Time of the Last Incas* (New York, Macmillan, 1962), also by Professor Baudin, gives a simple and out-of-date image of the Incas.

The best over-all study of the Incas is the article by John H. Rowe, "Inca Culture" (published by the Smithsonian Institution in the *Handbook of South American Indians,* Washington, Vol. 2, 1946), which has an excellent bibliography. The political and judicial institutions of the Incas are considered in detail by Sally Falk Moore, *Power and Property in Inca Peru* (New York, Columbia University Press, 1958). The little book by the American writer Victor W. von Hagen, *Realm of the Incas* (New York, Mentor Books, 1957), is not without merit despite its popular tone.

For the history of the Incas under Spanish rule, the reader is referred to the remarkable study by G. Kubler, "The Quechua in the Colonial World" *(Handbook of South American Indians,* Vol. 2, pp. 331–410); and to a long article by John H. Rowe in the *Hispanic American Historical Review* (Vol. XXXVII, No. 2, May 1957), under the title "The Incas under Spanish Colonial Institutions." As for the modern Indians of Bolivia and Peru, the remote heirs of the Inca civilization, they have been the subject of an increasing number of studies. To those who wish to form a general idea of their mode of life, one would suggest reading the article "The Contemporary Quechua" *(Handbook of South American Indians,* Vol. 2, pp. 411–470), and the monograph by Harry Tshopick, *The Aymara of Chacuito, Peru. I: Magic* (American Museum of Natural History Anthropological Papers, Vol. 44, Part 2, New York, 1951). Under the direction of José Matos, the Institute of Ethnology of the University of San Marcos, Lima, Peru, has published a series of studies on the Indian communities: *Las Comunidades de Indigenas de Huarochiri en 1955* (Lima, 1958).

The present state of our knowledge of the civilizations preceding that of the Incas is very clearly summed up in *Peru* by G. H. S. Bushnell (London, Thames and Hudson, 1956); and also in *The Ancient Civilisations of Peru* by J. Alden Mason (Harmondsworth, Penguin Books, 1957), which has a first-class bibliography.

Inca art, not nearly so rich as that of the Mochicas or of Nazca, has only a modest place in the illustrated works devoted to pre-Columbian art. The monograph by M. and Mme. d'Harcourt, *La Musique des Incas et ses survivances* (Paris, 1925) remains a classic, as does their other work *Textiles anciens du Pérou et leurs techniques* (Paris, 1924).

To understand the conquest of Peru, one must read William H. Prescott's masterpiece, *History of the Conquest of Peru* (New York, Modern Library, 1936), although the introduction on the civilization of the Incas is now out of date in many respects.